*I was incredibly surprised b*
*boring notes and newspape*
*an effort to create a story, t...*
almost demands you join the author as she pursues justice for a family that has encountered so many wrongs.

After a brief intro that sets the stage for the story and a little bit of background on the author that provides insight into why she dedicated a large portion of her life to a family that was nothing but strangers when she first met them, Gentilcore begins leading us down a dark and twisted path filled with numerous mysteries. I've read plenty of true crime books but I don't think I've ever seen justice so conveniently and expertly thwarted. As each new clue surfaces, you won't be able to resist asking yourself how such a think could occur.

You will feel the excitement of the feisty reporter that's busting with enthusiasm over the possibilities that are contained within this mystery, and you will still be right by her side as the weary journalist doggedly sticks to the path years later for no other reason than her desire to help this family that seems to have no other place to turn.

I love how the author holds nothing back. Our hero isn't a perfect and flawless creature that always has the answers. She's a real person that feels fear and doubt, sometimes using all her strength just to continue a fight that sometimes seems impossible to win. I also like how all the facts, evidence, and clues of the case are laid out for us, allowing the reader to put their detective skills to use in this quest for justice.

Five Stars. If you're a fan of true crime or mystery stories, you need to give "Justice Wanted: The Kid in the University Stairwell" a try. I guarantee you will never again look at quiet college towns the same.

–Marty Shaw, *Reader Views Book Review*

Truth doesn't always come so easily. "Justice Wanted" follows Marlene Gentilcore as she seeks the truth on the strange death of Jack Alan Davis, whose death was officially ruled choking to death on his own vomit after binge drinking. Questioning this verdict, Gentilcore finds much on the table to reinforce her suspicions, questioning the quick dismissal of the case. "Justice Wanted" is a fine read that offers much to think about in the modern pursuit of justice.

–John Burroughs, *The Midwest Book Review*

# JUSTICE WANTED

# JUSTICE WANTED

### THE KID IN THE UNIVERSITY STAIRWELL

### You Be the Judge.

## A QUEST FOR PROMISED JUSTICE IN AMERICA

Marlene Gentilcore

The publisher of this book is neither responsible for nor necessarily in agreement with the views of the author, facts presented by the author, or conclusions drawn by the author in this book. Though the publisher has every expectation that all research performed by the author for this book was done professionally and in good faith and has been honestly presented, the publisher can offer no such guarantees to the reader.

Back cover photograph of Jack Alan Davis, Jr. compliments of Elaine Davis-Lynch

Copyright © 2011 by Marlene Gentilcore

All rights reserved. No part of this book may be used or reproduced in any manner whatsoever without written permission of the author.

Printed in the United States of America.

ISBN: 978-1-59571-648-4

Library of Congress Control Number: 2011923840

Rose-Colored Publications
Pittsburgh, Pennsylvania

*In every child who is born,
under no matter what circumstances,
and of no matter what parents,
the potentiality of the human race is born again:
and in him, too, once more, and of each of us,
our terrific responsibility toward human life;
toward the utmost idea of goodness....*

JAMES AGEE

*This book is dedicated to…*

*My father, Lee, "The Author."*
*My mother, Catherine, "The Registered Nurse."*

*My children, their children, your children.*

*Jack Alan Davis, Jr. and his family.*

*And, to justice for all.*

# ACKNOWLEDGEMENTS

I would like to thank John Lynch for his courageous and dedicated effort to find truth and justice for his brother and family, and for believing in me. Without his determination, this story would not exist.

An extra special thanks to those not afraid to tell the truth.

Thanks to my friends and family for their constant support and for listening to me talk *ad nauseam* about this case for many years.

Finally, thanks to my mother for her constant encouragement and to my dear friend Mary Miller-Venturella for stepping up to help just in the nick of time.

# PREFACE

In 1987, I became a mother mourning her 20-year-old son, who died while away at college. Our family was led to believe that his death was just an unfortunate accident, but there was much more to it than we were told.

As the years went by, more information became available because of the caring and diligent writer/investigator, Marlene Gentilcore, and *Justice Wanted* is the story that unfolds.

Of course, it is still unfolding; and I still miss Jack every day. For those of you who believe, I feel him around me; there are times I smell him. I've even felt him hug me.

It would be nice to know the truth of what happened in October 1987. And my hope is one day someone will walk up to me and tell me why this happened to my son. Until then, I will be forever grateful to those involved for allowing us to find his body.

Elaine Davis-Lynch
March 3, 2004

# ONE

*An injustice anywhere is a threat to justice everywhere.*
Martin Luther King, Jr.

I had to do it. I knew I had to do it.

An investigator from the state Attorney General's office called and said I had to watch the videotape of the second autopsy. I'd read transcripts from both the first and second autopsies over and over many times. The first one sent me into battle, the second made me cry.

As an investigative reporter, my job is to find all the pieces of this case, put them together and hopefully come up with answers. So far, none of it was easy and nothing in my life up to this point had prepared me for the gruesome task before me.

Seeing eight-by-ten, black and white, glossy photos from the first autopsy was one thing; imagining what this boy would look like in living color on a 27-inch television screen in my living room after three long years underground scared the living hell out of me! I knew his face. He graduated from high school with my son.

Pictures of him stretched out on a cold, grey, stainless steel slab in the autopsy room the morning after his body was found are burnt into my brain forever. In some photos, he's still dressed in the plaid button-down shirt he borrowed from his roommate the night he disappeared. He's wearing ordinary, faded blue jeans and new, white, back-to-school sneakers. Other shots show him stripped naked with a huge dark, bloody hole carved into the space where his beautiful, young chest and vital organs should be.

When I finally mustered up enough courage to pick up the video of the second autopsy from the family's attorney, I felt relieved and very grateful to find this little audio cassette tape tucked under the larger video case in the bottom of the big, brown envelope. Their lawyer, who also needed to know the facts but apparently did not want to watch another human being dissected and mutilated in front of his eyes, recorded the sound track.

"Thank God, I don't have to watch the video. Thank God, I don't have to watch the video," became my mantra as I slowly crossed my living room, opened the plastic case, popped the cassette into the tape deck, and pushed PLAY. Recognizing sounds took a few minutes as my ears adjusted to strange banging noises. I stretched out on the floor with pen and paper in hand, determined to scribble down every word. Emotions could not get the best of me. I had to get through this tape to understand what an investigator at the Pennsylvania State Attorney General's office told me about this case.

My stomach muscles tightened. I could barely breathe as my ears honed in on each voice. Since I had worked on this case with world-renowned forensic pathologist Dr. Cyril Wecht for a few years, I recognized his voice immediately.

"Good preservation. Fair amount of hair is present on the forearms, thighs and forelegs. Higher half of the bony thorax and abdomen show no abnormalities. The pubic and external genitalia are normal adult male. The penis has not been circumcised. The upper and lower extremities show no deformities such that suggest fracture or dislocation. The soft body tissue of the hands are shrunken and dehydrated. No deformities of the fingers are noted. The fingernails are intact and evenly cut. The toenails are intact and evenly cut. The back is unremarkable. The skin of the back shows somewhat shriveled and lightly leathery in appearance but is intact. The skin and soft tissue of the entire body are in fairly well preserved condition, although the epidermis sloughs easily with slight pressure," Dr. Wecht dictates in his report.

"Debbie make a note, fit this paragraph in somewhere, I guess back to the beginning where the casket is mentioned. I may have already said, no separate bag or container is present within the casket containing the viscera."

"Just some cotton and sawdust," a voice says.

Dr. Wecht immediately identifies his assistant Joe and introduces him to those in attendance. "Sawdust material," Dr. Wecht says. "We don't have any organs, viscera."

"They went with the body to the funeral home," another voice says.

"There's nothing to be done about it," Dr. Wecht replies. "I know these things happen. If it's not there, it's not there. There is nothing we can do. Joe, we'll see if we can get another look at the testicle and we'll get a big hunk of ribs. So, why don't we take a look here first? Okay. All right. Take your time and we'll get all this stuff out. Probably need to get the tongue out, too. All right, fine. Then, we'll look. Then, we'll open the head and come down the back of the cervical spine."

"You're going to open the spinal cord?" Joe says.

My body stiffens as if in the dentist's chair waiting for the click and sudden shrill squeal of the drill. I press both hands over my ears to shut out the scream of the electric saw as it splits through the hard bone of his skull. It sounds worse than a million fingernails scraping across a slate chalkboard. I jump up and pace around my tiny living room, trying with all my might not to imagine Jack's child-like face.

He had very delicate facial features for a 20-year-old male. His dark blonde hair was cut in a shaggy 1980's kind of style in his high school senior picture. His deep blue eyes looked bright, enthusiastic. His thin lips gently curved into a warm, friendly, impish smile. He joined the track team and decided to major in business his freshman year at Indiana University of Pennsylvania.

"Tom, do you want to get a picture here?" Dr. Wecht says, matching the previously heard unidentified voice to a name. Thomas Streams, the Indiana County Coroner who handled the first autopsy. "That membrane is called the dura meter," Dr. Wecht says, describing Jack's brain. "On top of it where there is a hemorrhage, that is called the extradural or epidermal. Beneath it is called subdural. So, it's beneath the membrane but on top of the brain. Well, it's from injury. It's not spontaneous. But, I don't want to jump to conclusions.

"It's more consistent. Let me stop right there, you can get it from a blow or a fall. The other things you look for that help you in a fresh body and such, sometimes there are things like if there is a fracture. Just take your time because I want to be able to lay that down and orient it properly. So, I don't want to jump to conclusions yet as to the ideology of this, the cause. See that's the membrane. That's on the undersurface."

"How wide is the surface damage?" Coroner Streams asks.

"We'll take some measurements and describe its location," Dr. Wecht replies. "Tom, we'll set this brain down and you can take pictures. Get some larger containers. I want to show you the whole brain, of course. You see the hemorrhage?"

"How big is the hemorrhage?" Streams asks.

"This is a substantial hemorrhage. Don't forget we got shrunken tissues here and a lot of this is dried up. Here look," Dr. Wecht answers. "This is a big area. I'll turn it around. Here Tom and Carl (Pennsylvania State Trooper Carl Schwinberger) take your pictures. This is the brain stem here, back of the brain. This is on the left side. This is a wide substantial area. I can tell you this, this much I will say. I can already understand why he would have been incapacitated. Fuck! How it happened? Who the fuck knows! And where it happened I don't know. But I can understand one thing already, why he was incapacitated. Why he wasn't able to cry out or call out for help. And, you can't die right away from this."

"Do you want to take the whole cord," Joe says.

"Oh God! Oh God! Oh Jesus!" Dr. Wecht yells over the screaming saw now slicing through his spinal cord. " Look at that! That's hemorrhage in the fucking spinal cord. You're looking at spinal cord. Joe has lifted up the bone. That hemorrhage is in the Goddamn spinal cord! Let's take out the spinal cord."

My teeth hurt. I hold my ears, desperate to block out the horrific images again. Of course, when you are transcribing a tape you have to stop, rewind and play it over and over to make sure you've written down every word as accurately as possible. Just the memory of listening to this tape over and over that day brings tears to my eyes.

"Joe, take some more of that away. Wow! See what happens is the blood drips down from the head. See, very good, Joe. This is the spinal cord. See that soft stuff. If you were to feel it, you can feel it if you want. See, I'm wiggling it now. That is blood overlying it. Take your pictures. Then what we're going to do is cut the whole cord out and save it. We'll put that in a separate container, Joe. Well, the hemorrhage is staining in here, too. It's staining in the inside of the bone."

"We can take that vertebrate," Joe says.

"I think we will, too," Dr. Wecht said. "In fact, I think we will save this part. Just cut it off there, Joe."

"Anyone's wife sell Tupperware?" a voice says. "Maybe we've got a sale here."

Everyone laughs. Further along on the tape everyone chuckles about the odor.

"Could you close that door?" Joe says. "My clothes are in there and I don't want to take too much of this smell home with me."

"Don't worry, Joe. When it buys your kid a new car in a few years, he won't give a shit about the smell," Dr. Wecht says. "He'll say come home smelling a little more often."

Tears well in my eyes, spilling one by one down each cheek. Something inside me changes at that moment. His young face is gone. All that's left is a pile of raw flesh and severed bones where the bright promises, hopes and dreams of a young human life use to be.

"No! This is not the way it's supposed to be!" a voice screams inside my head. You'd think I'd be used to all the gut-wrenching twists and turns in this case by now, or maybe as some might say, my expectations were just too high.

# TWO

*It is we who nourish the soul of the world.*

PAULO CAELHO

"Your father raised you with rose-colored glasses," my mother said, shaking her head as if this was definitely not a good thing.

"What does *that* mean?" I thought, still young enough to picture myself wearing fancy red-framed eyeglasses with pink tinted lenses before she changed the subject.

Of course, being the kind of person I am, I looked up the definition, which left me wondering if I do have an idyllic view of the world. And if so, was it my dad's fault? And how exactly did he tint my world pink? I don't recall him doing or saying anything unusual. He whistled as he walked down the street on his way home from the bus stop after work and told jokes at the dinner table to make us all laugh. You felt good being around him.

If he had lived his childhood dream, I believe, my dad would've happily tap-danced his way across stage and screen, like Gene Kelly his idol and high school classmate. An air of lightness surrounded him; his smiles were contagious and his energy lit up the room. His thoughtfulness turned Christmas and other holidays into joyful magic for our family. He helped people find their smiles—not a bad legacy, if you ask me.

What's so bad about wanting to see others happy? How can seeing the world bathed in beautiful light be wrong? Perhaps frustrating and disappointing at times, but bad?

Of course, my father played an important role, as other fathers do, in shaping my world as a child. But he's not the only one who influenced, molded and filled my mind with high ideals. Looking back at my first childhood memory, I can pinpoint the exact moment these idyllic notions captured my brain.

I'm four years old, barely tall enough to peek over the top of the grey Formica tabletop of our 50's-style chrome kitchen set on tippy toes. My mother sits at one end sipping her cup of morning coffee.

"Why can't I go to school?" I beg, my body twisting in agony for emphasis. "I want to go to school with the other kids. *Ple-e-e-ease, Mom. Ple-e-e-e-ease.*"

"You're not old enough," she says, sweetly, as I recall, even though she must have been sick and tired of hearing my plea every morning for at least a year. "You have to be five-years-old to go to kindergarten. Pretty soon. You have to wait."

You know how one day seems so long when you're a child and waiting for anything—especially Christmas—feels like an eternity. Eventually, you learn you have no choice but to wait. Watching my older sister walk half a city block, cross the street, then disappear amongst kids of all ages running in every direction, playing games, laughing, yelling and having so much fun day after day in the red brick school yard, made me desperate. I wanted to go to school *so-o-o* bad. Instead I faced another day home alone with no one to play with.

You could see the kindergarten windows from the end of our street. They were always decorated with paste and cut artwork of all different colors, shapes and sizes, made by all the kids having fun in school, except me.

Of course, the day finally came to set off on my long-awaited adventure. My mother put my little hand in hers and we crossed that forbidden street together for my first half day at "big girl" school. Being so terrified and excited at the same time, I burst into tears and refused to stay as soon as we walked into the classroom. Boy, was my mom surprised!

To this day, she loves to tell and retell—especially to my children and grandchildren—all the details of my first traumatic day at school and how she had to strike a bargain with me to stay.

"She cried and carried on, even tried to run out the door!" she says, loving every minute. "The only way she'd agree to stay is if she could sit next to this one little boy and no one else."

I saw him as soon as we walked in the room. I'd never seen a person so beautiful, with skin the color of chocolate. My mother whispered in the teacher's ear. She smiled and simply pulled a tiny chair out for me to sit on right next to Eugene Banks. Of course, he never knew he played such an important role in my education or became the topic of discussion that morning. He sat quietly, totally absorbed in pushing a thick cord through the small holes in the middle of various wooden beads of all different shapes and colors scattered in front of him on the table. He never looked up or at me when I sat down next to him. Little did he know he did his good deed for the day.

"Class, pay attention now," said the teacher—whom I completely adored the second my mother walked out the door. "I want everyone to stand up straight and tall next to your chair. That's right. Good."

At that moment in time, our whole world revolved around being perfect.

"Now, hold your right hand up like this," she said, pointing with the other hand to kids still confused by right and left, including me. "Wonderful. Now, place your hand across your chest like this, about right here, in the middle over your heart."

Eager to please, we placed our tiny hands over our hearts, turned as instructed to face the small American flag in the front of the room hanging from a little wooden pole attached to the top of the door frame.

"Repeat after me," she said.

*"I pledge allegiance to the flag of the United States of America, and to the Republic for which it stands, one nation under God, indivisible, with liberty and justice for all."*

Granted those were pretty big words for five-year-olds to grasp, but we mumbled along doing our best because the tone of her voice implied serious business. Do you remember your first time? You didn't know what the words meant or why you had to say them but those questions never crossed your mind. You accepted taking the pledge as just a part of going to school.

Last summer, I went back to Dilworth Elementary School. Everything looked and felt the same after all these years, warm and comforting. This time, I stood alone in the smaller-than-I-remember now-quiet red brick schoolyard, full of wonderful and some not-so-great childhood memories. I picked out the kindergarten, library and principal's office windows as I slowly walked around the building and up the steps to the main entrance. The doors were locked for summer vacation so I craned my neck in several directions to peek through the windows.

"How I'd love to walk through those halls again," I thought, promising to return during the school year. As I turned around to head back down the steps, the gigantic flagpole—twice as tall as the school building—caught my eye. When I looked up and saw the enormous American flag at the very top waving slowly, majestically in the warm, gentle breeze, sweet memories came to life in my mind.

Every Friday morning, a small piano was rolled out into the hall and pushed up against the wall next to the main entrance opposite the principal's office. The music teacher's fingers flew across the black and white keys, playing one patriotic song after another as every student, kindergarten through eighth grade, marched two-by-two through the halls—careful to follow the white lines running down the middle of the mint green marble floors, out through the double doors of the main entrance, down the wide, cascading, cement steps and straight ahead about twenty yards to the enormous flag pole outside.

Marching in gym class was a part of our school curriculum. We were all taught to "square corners" with precision in preparation for the weekly ritual of parading through the halls past the principal's office. We strived to do our best. There was a lot at stake! The class that stepped in perfect unison to the music, maneuvered sharp corners and made it all the way to the end of the sidewalk inches in front of the flag pole—before partners split down the middle, one child veering right the other left at the same exact time—won the big prize!

If you walked into your homeroom Monday morning and saw this big beautiful flag from the principal's office with its long flowing red and white stripes gracefully draped in the corner— your class won! The flag looked so tall and majestic to us wee ones back then. The golden eagle with wings spread wide perched atop the polished, dark wooden flagpole reached all the way to the ceiling! The symbol of perfection, honor and victory! We performed the best that week.

Funny, a thought just crossed my mind for the very first time. I bet the principal made sure each class won every year. After all, kindergarten kids had to compete against eighth graders with years of experience under their belts. She had to be fair. Kind of sad to think no one actually won but maybe how well you marched didn't matter as much as the feeling of pride this school and this ritual instilled in all of us. We held our heads extra high, faces beaming each and every time we earned the honor of turning towards the magnificent American flag to repeat the words meant to live inside us forever.

One day in sixth or seventh grade, I stood next to my desk with my hand over my heart on one of those carefree elementary school days, repeating the same words I'd said so many times already, but this time—they sunk in! I actually listened to the words we'd all been saying out loud in unison day after day for years!

My first epiphany! A soul awakening! I'd been pledging loyalty to my country all this time and didn't have a clue! Click. A light went on in my head that lit up my entire face. At that exact moment, I understood the *Pledge of Allegiance*. Pride swelled inside my chest as the world changed right in front of my eyes. I was a part of something bigger than the child-size life around me. A country that promises freedom and justice for all! Wow!

I believed. We recited the pledge approximately 1,560 times from the first day of kindergarten to high school graduation day. I did; you did; we all did—including Jack Alan Davis, Jr. and his family. Little did we know as we set out on this incredible journey together, whether you look through rose-colored glasses or not, justice is something you have to fight for, just like that symbolic flag in grade school.

There were hard lessons to learn on the way to finding the truth, but I did not forget for one second the promise my country made to me as a child. Perhaps the betrayal I felt during this fifteen-year investigation came from my belief that justice is a right instead of a promise based on high ideals.

Not just any high ideals but those noble ones outlined by the forefathers of this country in the constitution. Talk about rose-colored glasses! They must have worn out several pairs as they gazed into the future on their quest to create a country unlike any other on the planet.

Maybe my mom was right, I do view the world through rose-colored glasses, and my gentle father did shape my perspective of the world—but he did not act alone. Oh, no. My country, aided and abetted by the likes of Thomas Jefferson, Benjamin Franklin, John Adams and a bunch of other guys including Francis Bellamy who wrote the pledge in 1892, molded my young, impressionable and innocent mind.

# THREE

*Nothing happens until something moves.*

ALBERT EINSTEIN

We were so naive and such innocents when we met. A mutual friend invited me to John and Marisa's house the week after Thanksgiving 1989. I still remember squeezing past the prickly branches of this big, fat, bushy, oddly shaped Christmas tree to get through the front door of their first-floor apartment. A hot fire blazed in the fireplace—I love fireplaces—casting a warm, orange glow over their small living room, very cluttered with toys. We sipped drinks, nibbled some snacks, and shared the usual polite, new-acquaintance chatter sprinkled with a few personal tidbits.

John worked as a landscaper, weather permitting, during the day and spent nights earning a baker's certificate at a local supermarket. Marisa, who looked more than ready to give birth to their second child, worked as an accountant for *Mister Rogers' Neighborhood*.

"You work for Mr. Rogers?" I said, surprised. "I watched Mr. Rogers for years with my kids and never pictured people actually working for him."

"My mother-in-law works for him, too," she said. "She started right out of high school and has been there ever since."

Marisa was on maternity leave and you could tell the prospect of giving birth right before Christmas weighed on her mind. We hit it off right away, talking about work, kids and the stress of getting ready for the holidays. John stood in the doorway yelling out a promise to let me know when the baby arrived as I made a mad dash down their driveway to get in my car and out of the cold.

I bought the cutest little fuzzy black- and brown- tiger-striped sleeper, complete with tiger ears and tail as soon as I heard the news. Their son was born about two weeks before Christmas. A few weeks into the New Year, I called to see about stopping by to see their new baby and give them my gift.

"You busy now? " John asked. "If not, come over."

When I knocked on the door he answered, ushering me into the dark living room lit only by the warm, orange glow of the fireplace. There's nothing cozier than a hot, blazing fire on a cold, winter night, right?

"Marisa's not back yet," he said. "She went shopping and took our other little one with her. I'm babysitting. He's sleeping right now. They should be back any minute."

John pointed to a straight-back, wooden chair with padded back and seat, directly across from the fire. I sat down, thinking this was not a very comfortable chair to have in your living room.

"Do you want something to drink?" he said, nervous, anxious, on edge. Of course, we were strangers at that point.

"Water's okay," I said as John vanished down the hall to the kitchen. He returned in seconds, handed me a glass of ice water and plopped down in the corner of the couch on my left. When I turned my head, his face was less then two feet away.

"So, I hear you're a reporter with the *Tribune-Review*," he said, starting our very awkward conversation.

"Well, sort of. I do freelance work," I replied, immediately explaining the difference out of habit. "I'm not an employee. I work on assignment and get paid per published story."

In turn, John explained how he managed baking bread and donuts all night on top of doing backbreaking landscape work during the day and still found time to sleep. We also talked about the baby and how well his three-year-old was adjusting to her new baby brother.

"They should be home any minute," John said, still nervous. "Can you stay until the baby wakes up? I know Marisa would like to see you again."

He didn't have to ask twice. The hot fire felt so good that frigid January night, so comfortable. I blabbed on about my recent divorce and my three children. I told their ages and that we had lived in Penn Hills for the past sixteen years.

"I've lived in Penn Hills most of my life and have seven brothers and sisters," John said. "Well, six now. Do you remember the kid they found in the stairwell up at IUP? That was my brother."

"That was your brother!" I said, my head snapping around, wide-eyes gawking, stunned.

Who in and around Pittsburgh or western Pennsylvania for that matter hadn't heard about his brother and the way he died? I remember the exact moment I heard about his freakish death. I was sitting on the couch in my mother's living room as our dinner simmered on the stove and she read the Sunday paper.

"Did you hear about the boy they found dead in a stairwell at that college?" she said, crumpling the corner of the newspaper down to expose the astonished look on her face. "He was from

Penn Hills, you know." She slowly turned her head from side to side saying, "What a shame," without words.

"They said he laid in that stairwell for five days. Can you believe it! Can you believe no one saw him laying right there in the stairwell for five days?" Her head now moved back and forth much faster. "They said he choked to death on his own vomit!" Her tongue was now clicking with each turn of her head. "What a shame," she said. "His poor parents."

"Where was the stairwell?" I said, trying to imagine a dead body lying in any stairwell and then picturing students rushing up and down the winding staircases between classes inside the Cathedral of Learning on the University of Pittsburgh campus. A body wouldn't go unnoticed five minutes–let alone five days.

I'd heard of Indiana State University of Pennsylvania, or IUP as locals call it, but never gave it much thought. It was just some college located in some small town somewhere north of Pittsburgh, which made the story sound even more bizarre.

How could a dead body go unnoticed on such a small campus? Now my head moved from side to side. It was hard to believe. He choked on his own vomit? Never heard of such a thing and it seemed physically impossible. What a strange way for someone so young to die.

"Did you hear about the kid they found in the stairwell up at IUP," my son said a few days later. "He went to Penn Hills High School. We graduated together." His head also turned slowly from side-to-side as he spoke. "Can you believe no one saw his body in that stairwell for five days? There's no way! That's impossible! I really didn't know him that well but he seemed like a nice kid."

"Actually, he was my step-brother," John said, eager to tell his story. "My mother died when I was eleven. Jack's mother married my father with seven kids."

"She must have been some kind of saint to marry someone with seven kids," I said, letting a few nervous, jerky laughs escape while thinking in the back of my mind that she must have been insane. After raising three kids of my own, it was hard to imagine any woman volunteering for that much responsibility, willingly.

"Well, I ended up taking care of the younger kids," he said. "I was the oldest. Elaine and my dad sort of did their own thing. You know what I mean."

Picturing eight kids running around the house, I nodded.

"Jack was the youngest. He was more like a son to me than a brother. He was about two years old when they got married. He was the baby in the family," John said, his voice growing louder with each word.

"You know, I don't think I've had a good night's sleep since he died. I have this constant pain in my neck," he said, reaching up to rub the back of his neck while twisting his head from side to side. "They said he was drunk and choked to death on his own vomit. I never believed what they said. I know my brother and he didn't drink that much. At least, I never saw him do it anyway."

As he spoke, I glanced down, noticing my hands moving slowly, rubbing back and forth over the worn-smooth surface on each arm of the old wooden chair. Every muscle in my body was now tense, on alert, ready to skyrocket through the roof or bolt out the front door.

"I never believed all the bullshit," he said, anger mounting. "My brothers went up there with his mother, father and stepmother to look for him. He was missing for five days. I didn't go." His voice trailed off as he turned away to stare into the fire. I didn't know what to say.

"The day he disappeared, me and Marisa started driving to Indiana for no reason. We got halfway there and turned around. Our daughter was just a baby then and we had groceries in the car. I wish we'd kept going that day; maybe none of this would have happened. His roommates called Monday to say he was missing. I didn't go with my brothers to search for him," he said again.

I sat mesmerized, unable to break away from his penetrating blue eyes, brightly lit by the yellow-orange glow in the dark room. He stared right through me as he ranted about Jack's fraternity brothers showing up at the funeral with black eyes and bruises, looking as if they'd been in a fight.

"I just don't believe he died the way they said he did," John said, his head turning slowly from side to side as he spoke. "Kids lined up almost around the outside of the funeral home. There were lots of people there. Oh, and get this! This priest—this asshole—pushes his way through the crowd, stands in front of Jack's casket and starts preaching about the evils of underage drinking! Can you imagine! Fucking asshole!"

I half listened for the baby to wake up crying in the next room.

"Jack was only twenty when he died. On his twenty-first birthday, Marisa and my sisters made a blanket out of pine tree branches. They wove them together and laid them on his grave. We poured a bottle of Jack Daniels over it. He wasn't even old enough to drink when he died!"

John sounded tough, streetwise, ready to kick ass. His red face and piercing eyes were only inches from my face. He looked like one of those scary faces you make by holding a flashlight under your chin in the dark on Halloween. I had to look away. I looked down at my hands, now grasping the wooden arms of the chair so tightly that my knuckles glowed white in the dark. I nodded, listened, listened, nodded. Until suddenly, all John's scattered thoughts gelled inside my brain and in a split second shot uncensored out of my mouth, "Are you saying your brother was murdered!"

He froze, staring straight into my eyes. All those endless crazy thoughts running through his head for the past two years put into words. I felt as if someone just poured ice water down my spine, into my bones. My entire body shivered despite the hot raging fire less than ten feet away. There was nothing left to say. We sat staring at the dancing flames for some time before the front door burst open, forcing in a gust of biting, cold wind; along with the sound of Marisa's voice to pierce the silence and break the spell.

John's daughter ran straight for her daddy's lap. Marisa huffed and puffed towards the dining room, lugging several plastic shopping bags and talking fast. She told the tale of countless mothers who attempt to try on clothes with toddlers in tow—until she turned and saw our faces. We must have looked like two wide-eyed kids sitting around a campfire telling ghost stores, which wasn't far from the truth.

"I was telling her about Jack," he said softly.

"Oh," she said, meeting his eyes with an uncertain but knowing look. She studied my face for a second, turned and quietly continued unpacking her bags.

"We saved everything we got our hands on when it happened," she said, without looking our way. "There was just something about the whole thing that never seemed right. We just can't believe he died the way they said he did."

I understood completely. I had a hard time believing the story myself. And who in their right mind wants to believe that a loved one drank himself into a stupor then choked to death on his own vomit? I also understood that my life up to that moment had not prepared me to deal with what happened next.

So far, I'd led a pretty sheltered life. Married five days after my sixteenth birthday, raised three children in the suburbs most of my life, trained as a registered nurse, worked as a nurse, changed my mind and spent thirteen years earning a degree in journalism part-time. My recent divorce forced me into dealing with three angry teenagers while learning how to survive on my own in the world after having been married since childhood.

I covered monthly municipal and school board meetings, plus wrote advertising copy on a weekly basis as well as an occasional feature story to make ends meet over the past three years. So, investigating a murder was way—*way*—out of my league.

"Did you know she is a reporter?" John said, glancing sideways at Marisa, who took a seat next to him on the couch.

"Do you want to see what we have?" she said, standing to go get it.

"Maybe some other time," I said also standing but moving towards the door with my insides still trembling, my skin cold and clammy, and my brain off somewhere floating in space. In other words, I was in shock!

I had never known anyone who was murdered or even known someone who knew someone who was murdered. Let alone someone related to a murder victim. I tried desperately to shut John's angry voice and penetrating eyes out of my mind on

33

the way home that night and every night until I went back for more.

They didn't seem the least bit surprised to see me standing unannounced at their front door a week later. Marisa walked into the bedroom without uttering a single word and returned dragging two, white, plastic grocery bags filled with papers behind her.

"Like I said, we saved everything we could get our hands on when it happened," she said, dropping the bags at my feet. "I think the autopsy report's in there, too."

I reached into one bag, felt around and pulled out some papers. "Lucky me," I thought, staring at the words, "Autopsy Report."

John sat on the floor in front of me holding the baby comfortably between his outstretched legs. Marisa sat opposite him holding their daughter the same way. They may have exchanged words; the kids might have made noise. I never heard. Every time I glanced up from the page, two sets of searching, waiting eyes met mine.

Maybe they knew, maybe they didn't know, I had no idea what the hell I was doing. Maybe at this point they didn't care that I'd never seen an autopsy report before. To top it all off, I had to sit on their couch in their living room reading this detailed description of how the body of the person they loved was dissected piece by piece.

I recognized medical terms and body parts, no problem. Dealing with reality, already a problem. Every time the thought hit me that this mutilated body belonged to John's little brother, a person he spent Christmas mornings opening presents with, laughed and cried with, and now mourned, I couldn't breathe.

"You're a reporter," I repeated to myself over and over, sucking air through my nose and into my lungs. "You can do this. Be objective. Reporters have to be objective."

Food particles found in the throat and lungs sounded normal, considering he choked to death on his own vomit. Nothing out of the ordinary, the report even described which side of the head his hair was parted on. It looked like a thorough examination to me. What did I know? The only thing that finally caught my eye was the time of death.

"Did anyone ever notice there are two times of death listed here?"

"No," they said in unison. John slowly turned his head from side to side with the words, "I knew it!" written on his face.

"The coroner wrote that he died at two o'clock Saturday morning, but the pathologist, who performed the autopsy, recorded the time of death as two o'clock Sunday morning."

Their wide eyes now focused on me like lasers.

"That's a twenty-four-hour difference. It may not be significant, maybe just a mistake. As I said, I don't know too much about this stuff. But it does seem like a pretty big time difference when you're talking about a dead body," I said, feeling totally uncomfortable about saying anything else at this point. "Do you mind if I take this stuff with me to look at when I have more time?"

The bags were in my arms and out the door in minutes. I guess they figured if I worked with one of the largest newspapers in town, I must know exactly what to do with this stuff. Then again, maybe they just wanted someone to take the nightmare out of their bedroom closet.

"My step-mother never wanted to look into this," John said, walking next to me down the driveway to my car. "I don't think she can handle it. We can't tell her what we're doing. I want to know though. I don't think they told us the truth."

What were we doing? I drove away with their suspicions and now mine. Little did I know, at that moment, my life changed forever. Even as I type these words today, the memories feel so unreal.

In less than an hour, I sat in the middle in my living room floor with the contents of both bags scattered around me on the floor. Searching the old newspaper clippings for dates to create some kind of time-line seemed the logical first step.

Was it true? Was John's brother murdered?

Why were two different times of death listed on the autopsy report? How was the time of death determined? I scribbled notes, jotted down questions, and started a list with "Call Indiana County Coroner" at the very top.

# FOUR

*Let me tell you the secret that has led me to my goal.
My strength lies solely in my tenacity.*

Louis Pasteur

Honestly, would you have been able to scan all the headlines, arrange a big pile of newspaper clippings in chronological order, then turn the lights out and go to bed? With the words *"STUDENT MISSING"* in big bold letters next to a picture of this young, happy face smiling up at you?

> *Indiana Gazette, October 19, 1987*
>
> *Indiana Borough police are investigating the report of missing person, Jack Alan Davis, Jr., a 20-year-old male who was last seen Saturday morning.*
>
> *Davis, an IUP student was seen shortly after midnight at Al Patti's bar in Indiana.*
>
> *"We've checked with everybody we could think of, and nobody has seen him since Saturday morning," Detective Sgt. Anthony Antolik said. "We're hoping someone that has seen him after he left Al Patti's will contact us."*
>
> *"Davis is 5 feet 9 inches tall and weighs 160 pounds. He has brown hair, blue eyes and a small scar below his left eye," police said.*

> When last seen he was wearing stone-washed jeans, a gray and red striped shirt, white tennis shoes and a Sigma Tau fraternity jacket."

A majority of the newspaper articles came from the town's local paper, the *Indiana Gazette*. The next one on top of the pile reported his body found at ten-twenty on the night of Wednesday, October 21 at the bottom of a stairwell outside the science building, following a search of the area by police and students.

Apparently, another student had last seen him on campus near the stairwell around one-thirty on the morning of October 17.

An autopsy was performed from 9:45 to 11:45 a.m. on Thursday, October 22 at the local hospital. Indiana County Coroner Thomas Streams ruled out foul play by noon the same day.

> *Indiana Gazette, October 22, 1987*
>
> "The death of the Penn Hills resident was caused by asphyxiation due to the aspiration of stomach contents, meaning he probably inhaled his own vomit," Streams announced at a press conference that afternoon. He set the time of death at 2 a.m. Saturday, October 17.
>
> "There is no indication of any violence or that Davis had fallen into the stairwell. There was only one minor hematoma above the left eyebrow of the victim. "

The coroner theorized Jack walked down into the stairwell, collapsed due to an unusually high content of alcohol, then regurgitated. Indiana Borough Police Detective Sgt. Antolik told reporters that there was no indication he had been drinking in any local establishment. Instead, he had been drinking at a private house party and the matter was under investigation.

> "A search for the missing student never entered my mind," Antolik told reporters. "Due to the amount of foot traffic in that section of campus and workmen who are constantly through that area, I deemed a search was not necessary. Due to the length of time Davis was missing, I thought someone had grabbed him or he had been kidnapped."

In the same article, the IUP Public Safety Director said,

> "Weyandt Hall is checked once or twice each evening but that stairwell is not checked since it is not a Weyandt Hall entry. Outside areas such as that stairwell are security-checked on a random basis."

Davis's body was found at night, in the dark, at the bottom of an outside stairwell police claim workmen use constantly and campus security claims is checked randomly. Strange, I thought, scanning the rest of the article until words about a "fight" between two fraternities the Friday night Jack disappeared caught my eye.

> "What had been termed a fight was just a shouting match," said Dr. David DeCostner, IUP Vice President of Student Affairs. "Davis was a member of the Sigma Tau Gamma fraternity, one of the groups reportedly involved in the shouting match."

There was a fight! I could still see the anxious look on John's face earlier that night as he described Jack's fraternity brothers showing up at the funeral home with black eyes and bruises. "No one can tell me they weren't in some kind of fight," he had said as we sat by the fire. Even if it did turn out to be more than a "shouting match" and Jack was involved, how did he end up in the bottom of that stairwell?

I quickly glanced up at the clock to calculate how many hours of sleep I could catch if I went to bed right now, even though the possibility of sleeping seemed absurd. Enough adrenalin coursed through my body to run the New York marathon without blinking an eye.

Another big, bold headline with the same picture of Jack smiling drew me to the next article.

> *Pittsburgh Press, October 23, 1987*
>
> *MOTHER SITES TRAGIC EXAMPLE TO PEERS*
>
> *The mother of an Indiana University of Pennsylvania sophomore who died after a night of heavy drinking says she hopes his classmates and other young people will benefit from her son's tragic example.*
>
> *"It doesn't seem to do any good for us as parents to get up on a soapbox and tell our kids, 'don't drink.' They have to find out for themselves," Elaine Lynch said yesterday.*
>
> *"My son's death is a tragic way for other kids to learn a lesson, but maybe now some of them won't make the same mistake."*
>
> *Sgt. Anthony Antolik of the Indiana Borough Police Department said his investigation shows Davis had been drinking at a private party off campus.*
>
> *Antolik said Davis drank beer and liquor for about three hours last Friday night.*
>
> *"Laboratory tests are also being conducted to determine the alcohol content of Davis' blood," said Coroner Streams.*

*Antolik said Davis was last seen alive between 1:00 and 1:30 a.m. Saturday at School Street and Oakland Avenue, an intersection near Weyandt Hall.*

*Explaining why Davis' body had gone undiscovered for nearly five days, Antolik said, "I don't think 50 percent of the population on this campus knew it (the stairwell) was there."*

*The stairwell leads to a mechanical room in the building, and maintenance personnel don't even use the stairs very often, university officials said.*

*Mrs. Lynch said she will visit Indiana's campus in the near future and "try to help the kids cope with the grief of losing a classmate they loved."*

I hadn't met the woman yet, but already admired her. Two days after her only natural-born child was found dead, she found enough strength to speak out against underage drinking to help other students. Where did she find the strength? I don't think I could have done it.

"She must be an incredible woman," I thought, shaking my head in disbelief as I moved to the next article.

*Indiana Gazette, October 23, 1987*

*HE WAS SOMEBODY'S SON, FRIEND...*

*Friends of Indiana University of Pennsylvania Jack Allan Davis, Jr. remain puzzled over the chain of events that led to the discovery of his body Wednesday night.*

*One of Davis' roommates, 20-year-old Scott Battlaglini, said Thursday that he and three other residents of 1243 Oakland Ave. first noticed Davis's disappearance Saturday night.*

"He was supposed to go to work Saturday for a friend of ours, and he didn't show up," Battlaglini said. "We thought that maybe, with his car, he went on a road trip, but even then he would've called."

Battlaglini said he and the other roommates were worried Sunday night, when no signs of Davis were present in the house. It wasn't until Monday, however, when Davis missed an entire day of classes, that the roommates started asking around campus and filed a missing-persons report with Indiana Borough police shortly before midnight.

"He hadn't been anywhere," Battlaglini said. "And he's real picky about his car."

The automobile, a 1987 two-toned black and gray cougar, was found Tuesday morning near Fox's Pizza Den on Oakland Avenue. Davis reportedly attended a party Friday night at a nearby house on Washington Street.

"He was too particular about the car to leave it anywhere," said roommate Kevin Berenzansky, 20, of Armagh.

"He parked it out of the way so that they (residents of the house) wouldn't bitch to have it moved," added another roommate, Tom Romeo, 19, of Clyde.

At that point, the roommates said they were frustrated and upset about Davis' long disappearance and alerted some of his fraternity brothers and family.

"We called as many people as we could," Berezansky said.

"We didn't want to worry the parents," Battlaglini said. "But, I didn't think he would be in Indiana."

Davis' roommates thought that Indiana police might have waited too long before conducting a search of the area, Berezansky said.

It wasn't until Davis' parents and family arrived Wednesday evening and initiated their own search that borough police lent a hand in organizing the search crew, he added.

"We just tried to look in all the places people might not have noticed on campus," Berezansky said.

The crew checked out creeks, fields and lots before fraternity members found Davis' slumped body at the bottom of an outdoor stairwell of Weyandt Hall near the intersection of Oakland Avenue and 10th Street.

Streams said at a news conference on Thursday that Davis' death was accidental. The autopsy showed no signs of foul play, he said, and Davis apparently walked down into the dark and seldom-used stairwell of his own volition.

Although no criminal arrests are pending, borough police Sgt. Anthony Antolik said an investigation into the events that led to the death will continue.

"He's somebody's son, somebody's brother and somebody's friend," said John Augustine, 23, who pledged the fraternity with Davis. "He was always there for people. It really hurts."

"He was a really nice guy. I'm going to miss him. Now, every time you walk past Weyandt Hall, you'll think about Jack," said Augustine.

That's enough, I thought, crawling into bed and wrapping myself up in blankets, determined to get at least a few hours sleep. I squeezed my eyes shut in an attempt to force myself to sleep, only to see all these strange faces, words and dates spinning around in my head. All of a sudden, I jumped out of bed, ran straight to the stack of newspaper clippings and flipped to the bottom of the pile. I had to find out how the story ended.

> *Indiana Gazette, January 13, 1988*
>
> *TESTS CONFIRM ACCIDENTAL DEATH RULING*
>
> *Final results of the autopsy and toxicological testing conducted in the case of former Indiana University of Pennsylvania student, Jack Alan Davis, Jr. confirm the death of the Penn Hills man was accidental.*
>
> *Indiana County Coroner Thomas L. Streams today released the results of the test stating that the manner of death was accidental in nature and that Davis, 20, died as a result of asphyxiation due to aspiration of gastric contents.*
>
> *The final report also confirmed that alcohol was a contributing factor in this death, Streams said. But he noted that the exact level of alcohol could not be determined.*

It was true. Now, the question you're probably asking yourself right now is, "How did the coroner announce Jack was intoxicated in October before the blood test results came back in January, three months later?"

An experienced investigator might have picked up on the discrepancy immediately. As for me, the novice investigative reporter, I was back in bed with the covers pulled over my head, desperate to sleep.

I'm not sure I slept at all that night but I was up and on the phone ready to talk to the Indiana County Coroner by nine the next morning. I had many questions. Like, for instance, how is time of death in any case determined? Is there some scientific procedure a coroner follows? What about the two times of death listed on the autopsy report? Which, theoretically, meant Jack may have been alive somewhere for twenty-four hours after supposedly consuming enough alcohol to render him unconscious and choke to death on his own vomit.

The coroner's answering machine picked up. I left my name and number. In the meantime, I figured, what the heck? I might as well get in touch with the pathologist whose name was listed on the autopsy report, Dr. Stephen Griffin. The operator at Indiana Hospital immediately switched my call. Dr. Griffin picked up. Everything happened so fast; I had to stop and think of my own name. Finally, I managed to identify myself as someone looking into the death of Jack Alan Davis, Jr. for his family.

"Can you tell me how you determined the time of death in this case?"

"You'll have to talk to Coroner Streams," the doctor said abruptly. "He determines the time of death." Click. He hung up! I held the phone away from my ear, staring at it just like in the movies. A doctor never hung up on me before!

Within minutes, the phone rang. Coroner Streams was on the other end. I identified myself, and then quickly asked about the two times of death in case he hung up on me, too.

"No one can determine the exact time of death in any case," the Indiana County Coroner said. "What Dr. Griffin wrote is a mistake. I based my time of death on the last time Jack had been seen alive by a student that night. Also, that student said that Jack was heavily intoxicated when he saw him."

What? I didn't know what else to say. A student said that Jack was intoxicated the night he disappeared, and his time of death is based on the last time this same student saw him alive?

"Who was this student? How did he get so much power?" I thought after our conversation ended. "What about evidence?"

I'd seen enough cops shows and news programs to know there's more to investigating an untimely death than someone's word. If that's how this coroner determined Jack was intoxicated at the time of death, what made him so sure Jack walked down those steps on his own in the middle of the night? Did Jack search for the stairwell in the dark, manage to walk to the bottom, then was so intoxicated that he puked and choked to death on his own vomit?

"This is crazy," I thought, picking up the phone to call Indiana Borough Police. The dispatcher switched me to the now Chief of Police, Anthony Antolik. I stated my business.

"Once the body was found on campus the case fell under the jurisdiction of the university," Antolik explained. "IUP police conducted the investigation. You'll have to call them."

Again, I was surprised. It's fair to say that from this point on just about everything surprised me. I didn't know university police had the authority to investigate deaths. I thought they dealt mainly with campus security.

I immediately called IUP police and talked to the investigator in this case. Introductions out of the way, I asked him how to go about getting a copy of his police report.

"Go to the state attorney general's office," he said. "That's the only way you'll get a copy of this police report. It's not public information; that's state law."

I thanked him, hung up, flipped through the phone book, found the number, and dialed the Pennsylvania Attorney General's office in Harrisburg.

"Why did they tell you to call here?" asked the perplexed woman who answered the phone. "It's up to the university to release that report. If the investigation is closed, I don't see any reason why that information would not be given out."

If this had been a cartoon, you'd have seen a gigantic question mark floating above my head right about now. Exasperated, I redialed the phone.

"The university is never going to release this report," the IUP officer said. "If you want, we can set up an appointment to review the report. I'd be happy to do that for you." I thanked him again and promised to call back. I decided to talk to John first to see if he wanted to go with me, and if so, when he might be able to get away before making an appointment.

The day started out strange and ended even stranger. After dinner, I tracked down a phone number for one of Jack's roommates who had been featured in the article about his friends. Maybe he could shed some light on this already confusing story—or make it more confusing.

"I don't feel right talking to you without the family's consent," he said. I hung up, and immediately called John to explain. He in turn called the student then called right back.

"He'll talk to you now," John said, "He's waiting for you to call back. Call me when you're finished."

"I can see the science building from the window of my new apartment," the former roommate said. "I think of his body laying down in that stairwell every time I look at that building. I don't believe he went into that stairwell alone. Did you get a copy of the toxicology report? You should get it. I'd like to know what it says. I think cocaine is involved. Jack didn't do cocaine."

He recalled the time Jack tried the drug and it made his heart beat so fast it scared the hell out of both of them. He talked about their friendship, saying they grew apart once Jack pledged the fraternity.

"I didn't like those guys. His big brother in the fraternity is known as the biggest cocaine dealer on campus," he said. "Get the toxicology report and let me know what you find. I'd really like to know. I don't trust any of those guys. There is this one guy, Tom Brennan, he's supposed to be the last person to have seen him alive. At least that's what I heard. He walked Jack back to campus that night. I know the guy and I wouldn't trust him as far as I can throw him. I will say this, I do not believe Jack went into that stairwell alone."

He made me promise a few times before he'd hang up to let him know when I had a copy of the toxicology report.

"I'll help you as much as I can and so will his other friends—as long as we're not identified. I have to live up here, you know."

What did that mean? Why did he sound scared?

I called John back to tell him what was said and make plans for the first of our many trips to Indiana the next morning.

"Are you ready for this?" I said. "It already sounds pretty crazy."

"More than ready," he said. "I just want to know the truth."

# FIVE

*There's nothing so finely perceived and so finely felt as injustice.*

CHARLES DICKENS

Four of us jumped into the light blue Chrysler minivan parked in John's driveway, around eight the next morning, eager to make the first sixty-mile trek to Indiana. We had recruited volunteers overnight to help with the legwork. John and his brother Mike sat up front; my daughter and I rode in back.

Tension was, as the saying goes, so thick you could cut it with a knife. John drove. Mike and my daughter stared out separate windows, watching the snow-covered scenery whiz by as I rechecked my list of things to accomplish that day for the umpteenth time, while trying not to lose my breakfast as the van sped up, down, around and over miles of windy country roads.

"I went down into the stairwell to see Jack when they found his body," Mike said, turning to look at me about halfway through our otherwise silent trip.

"It must have been very hard for you," I said. No reply. He stared out the window. We all knew without saying that our first stop would be the infamous stairwell.

As soon as John turned the van into the small town and headed toward campus, Mike pushed the van door open, jumped out in the middle of the street and took off running without saying a word.

"This is hard for him," John said, sounding calm but looking as shocked as we were. "He went down into the stairwell to see Jack that night. This is the first time he's been back."

He parked the van directly across from the red brick, V-shaped wall that marks the main entrance of the Indiana University of Pennsylvania campus. The six-foot wall extends only a short distance on both sides from the center opening; gigantic lanterns sit atop the main pillars on both sides.

Since we didn't know exactly where we were headed, we strolled through the ornate passage in the center of the red brick wall. Inside, several quaint red brick buildings form a semi-circle around a large courtyard. Students walked in every direction carrying books and toting heavy backpacks across the grassy space, completely ignoring the sidewalks that outline the square.

"There it is!" John said, pointing to the first building on our left. The three of us stood directly in front of Weyandt Hall but could not see the stairwell, and no sidewalk or path marked the way. We walked to the left through the grass around the corner of the building, past tall green bushes on our right, before noticing a red metal handrail sticking out of the top of the stairwell on the left side; Mike was standing there alone, staring down into the hole.

"I went down there and touched his chest and shoulder. They were hard," he said, turning his face away to sniff back tears. "There was blood coming out of his nose and mouth. I remember thinking Jack's nose was swollen like it might be broken."

The stairwell looked a lot bigger than I had imagined. Fifteen concrete steps led down to a middle landing about ten feet in length, then five more steps led down to the bottom. If you extended your arms straight out on both sides of your body and walked down, you'd touch the red brick building on the right and a massive concrete wall on the left. You feel as if you're walking down into a gigantic hole in the ground surrounded by twenty-foot walls.

Looking up, you can see three floors of classroom windows overhead on the right, as well as directly above the back wall of the stairwell. "DANGER" is posted in big red letters on the gray, steel door on the right at the bottom of the steps. With a slight push, the door opened into a dark basement, which university officials identified as a maintenance room in one of the newspaper articles. They also told reporters the door was kept locked.

The unlocked door surprised us, as did the number of windows directly above the stairwell. Standing there in broad daylight in the exact spot where Jack's body was found made the possibility of his body going unnoticed for five days seem impossible.

Of course, the fact that a person would have to make a serious effort to find the stairwell—especially in the dark—crossed all our minds. Short bushy green shrubs line the outside perimeter of the stairwell that faces away from the building toward the street. So, if you're standing pretty much anywhere and look at the side of the science building, all you see are shrubs.

It's great place to hide—if you can find it! There's even a round cement pond-like fountain in front of the bushes. Jack's roommate's words echoed in my ears as I studied the area, "I can tell you he didn't go down there alone."

This was the first time John had seen the stairwell and I thought he was handling the situation well until he turned to speak to me. His face was so red I expected to see steam shoot out of his nose, mouth and both ears. Instead, he stood shouting idle threats at the university at the top of his lungs. At least I thought they were idle threats. I didn't know him well enough to be sure.

Either way, I thought it best to redirect our energy towards having a more productive day. I sent the two brothers off to clock the time it takes to walk from the bar Jack supposedly visited the night he disappeared, back to the stairwell. Next, they had to find the coroner's office and pick up a copy of the toxicology report. My daughter and I would head across campus to do research in the university library—but first I had to take a look through a couple of the classroom windows directly above the stairwell.

We went inside the first-floor classroom, walked to the back to look out windows to our right, and noticed a pencil sharpener attached to the sill directly above the target. I stood turning the handle casually pretending to sharpen a pencil. If I made an effort and leaned forward far enough—which meant bending over the wide ledge with the edge digging into my stomach—I could see into the bottom of the stairwell. Not exactly a natural pose for sharpening a pencil.

No need to check windows on upper levels since it was hard to see down into the gigantic hole from the first floor. Plus, time was running out. We had to get moving in order to accomplish everything on my list in only a few hours. John and I had to be back in time to go to work.

My daughter and I spent the next hour searching back issues of local newspapers and flipping through old yearbooks in the library. We copied a few articles and jotted down as many fraternity brother's names as possible before heading back to meet John and Mike. They seemed to be involved in a deep discussion about something until they saw us approach and came running.

Sideview of Weyhandt Hall from university's main campus entrance on Oakland Avenue. Stairwell entrance behind fountain and bushes.
(Photograph by Marlene Gentilcore)

Close-up of side of science building showing shrubs that adorn and block view of top of stairwell's 20-foot walls.
Arrow indicates entrance into stairwell.
(Photograph by Marlene Gentilcore)

Looking down into the 20-step stairwell with 15 steps to the 10-foot landing in the middle, and then 5 more steps to the bottom.
(Photograph by Marlene Gentilcore)

"It took twenty minutes for us to walk across town," Mike said as John waved sheets of white paper in my face.

"He asked why we wanted it! What nerve! I wanted to say, 'Because he is my brother, you asshole!' But instead I said, 'What's it to you?' He did ask who the lady was that called him—meaning you," he said, pointing his finger in my face. "I told him you were my sister! What business is it of his?"

I grabbed the toxicology report out of his hand and started reading as soon as the side door of the van slid shut. I had answers within minutes.

"It's true, John, cocaine was found in his body at the time of death," I said cautiously, not knowing how his brothers might react to the news.

"How did he know?" John said, referring to Jack's former roommate. I wondered, too. As soon as I walked through my front door and dropped an armload of papers on the table, I dialed the phone, hoping the kid would pick up.

"I told you," he said in a somber tone. "I want to talk to John now."

I hung up and waited—but not for long—before the phone rang.

"He said to concentrate on the fraternity," John said between frantic breaths. "He believes Jack's body was moved into the stairwell after he was dead. The fraternity Jack joined was not a real fraternity. They lost their national charter and were kicked off campus for fighting. He said he would help as much as he can if not identified."

I waited, expecting him to vent his anger as usual but he spoke softly.

"I knew something was wrong. I just knew it for such a long time," John said, sadly. It was late. We were both exhausted after a very stressful day.

"Good night, John," I said, matching his tone. "Get some sleep."

"I have to work," he said. "It's better this way. I won't have time to think."

I stretched out on the living room rug with a hot cup of chamomile tea to settle my stomach, determined to dissect and decipher the toxicology report piece by piece. Fortunately, I still had my medical dictionary from nursing school. Finding the definitions proved easy; understanding how specific substances in various amounts interact in a dead body went way over my head.

After studying the three-page report for hours, the date stamped on the report caught my eye. Coroner Streams received the report on December 23, 1987. I rechecked the date of the coroner's inquest in one of the newspaper articles. He received the report in December but did not release results to the family or public until January 13. Why'd he wait so long?

Nothing else in the report stood out except the statement, "a metabolite of cocaine was found indicating the use of cocaine, however, presence of the metabolite in the blood without the parent compound makes it difficult to accurately define the influence of this substance on an individual."

The fact that byproducts of the drug were found in his body after hearing about Jack's physical reaction to cocaine seemed odd. Then again, maybe he decided to try the drug again for some reason. No traces of marijuana were present and alcohol "ND*." I scanned the three-page report trying to find out what the initials stood for and found the answer on the last page, "*NONE DETECTED." What? What!

I sprang off the floor like my underpants caught fire and frantically paced back and forth through the three little rooms of my apartment, reading the words out loud over and over to myself. I couldn't believe my own eyes and ears! There it was in black and white—NONE DETECTED. NO ALCOHOL DETECTED! NO ALCOHOL FOUND IN HIS BLOOD AT THE TIME OF DEATH! My body shivered, trembled, shook.

What did this mean? How could it be? There must be some mistake. How did the Indiana County Coroner announce the toxicology report concluded that Jack was intoxicated at the time of his death—when there was no alcohol! And, if there was no alcohol, how in the world did he pass out and choke to death on his own vomit?

"He couldn't have!" screamed the voice inside my head.

I desperately wanted to call John but it was too late. Get a grip, I thought. You can't say anything to anyone until you're positive you know what you're talking about. There must be a logical explanation or some other scientific facts to consider.

Still, how could the coroner conclude Jack was intoxicated when there was no alcohol in his blood? Did he lie? That was impossible! How could he stand in front of this family, the press and tell a bold face lie with the truth printed right in this report? Now nothing made sense. I needed a second opinion—and fast!

I tossed and turned for what seemed like all night but must have dozed off at some point because I awoke with the answer. I looked up the number, picked up the phone and dialed the Allegheny County Coroner's office in Pittsburgh as soon as I finished brushing my teeth. A receptionist switched the call to someone she identified as the Deputy County Coroner.

I told him I was writing a term paper to avoid questions, then read the amounts of alcohol found in the stomach, blood and urine.

"Would this person be considered intoxicated at the time of death with these amounts of alcohol in his system," I said, holding my breath.

"If it says no alcohol was detected in the blood at the time of death, that person could not have been intoxicated when he died. Even after twenty days, the amount consumed would be found in the blood. It does not evaporate or deplete."

He also explained the properties of cocaine, saying the substance breaks down in the blood in approximately twelve hours but it takes three to six days to remove by-products out of the body through urination.

After a slight pause, the deputy coroner wondered if he could ask me a question. "How did this person have alcohol detected in his stomach and urine but not in the blood? It's the middle of the system. When you drink beer, it goes into your stomach through your bloodstream and is eliminated through urine."

He asked me to read the specific amounts again.

"The amounts of alcohol in the stomach and urine are insignificant," he said, muttering under his breath about how and why not even a tiny amount was found in the blood. "It's physically impossible for alcohol to be found in the stomach and urine but not in the blood. That's the middle of the system! Who did this report?"

Stunned by his reaction, I answered his question then thanked him for his time. He must have thought I was nuts! The words, "NOTE: Additional testing is being performed" typed at the bottom of the toxicology report took on new meaning after our conversation, so I contacted the lab.

After being switched from person to person, a supervisor at Roche Laboratories in Columbus, Ohio picked up the phone. Much to my surprise, as soon as I mentioned Jack's name, he instantly recalled the specifics of this two-year-old case.

"That was a strange situation," he said. "I suggest you talk to the doctor who sent the specimens. We only work with what we are sent. I do remember the case because we kept it for more testing. They were so mad at us because it took so long for us to send the results back."

All tests were performed as requested, he added. "If the report states that alcohol was not detected, it means it definitely was tested and no alcohol was found."

He assured me all test results were sent out together, then refused to say more and referred me to Dr. Griffin again. Feeling a bit overwhelmed, I decided to regroup before placing another call.

The blood had definitely been tested. No alcohol had been found. The lab conducted more tests to try and explain the results, which held up the report. Who was mad because it took so long to get the final results? The family? The pathologist? The Indiana County coroner who waited almost a full month to disclose the long-awaited final results?

"Are you sitting down, John?" I said on the phone that night. "I have something to tell you and it's not going to be easy. I talked to the coroner's office in Pittsburgh this morning to confirm my findings and make absolutely sure what I'm about to tell you is true." Deep breath. "John, no alcohol was detected in Jack's blood at the time of his death."

Not a peep. His breath stopped, then he let out a long, slow, steady stream of air. "What does that mean? What are you saying?"

My stomach clenched. I felt nauseous.

"It means he wasn't drunk when he died, John." Silence.

"Then how did he die?" John said almost in a whisper. "How did he die?"

"I don't know," I said, waiting in the silent calm before the storm.

"I should take some of my big friends up there. I'd get some answers—you better believe it! I'll get a gun and take some of those assholes out into the woods. Those bastards will tell the truth with a gun pointed at their fucking heads!"

I saw his bright red face and bulging blue eyes through the phone. One day, I'd get used to his anger. At that point, however, his temper still scared me even though I understood. He had every right to be pissed. I'd have been ranting and raving too.

"That's not going to solve anything," I said, thinking somewhere in the back of my mind, "Maybe he's right."

"Fry 'em!" he said. "We're going to fry those son of a bitches!"

"There's probably an explanation," I said. "We need more answers."

"Thank you," he said calmly.

"You're welcome," I replied, ending the first of many hard phone calls made during this case.

"How's anyone going to explain their way out of this one?" I wondered, climbing into bed.

# SIX

*Never give in. Never, never, never, never.
In nothing great or small, large or petty—never give in
except to convictions of honor and good taste.*

Winston Churchill

I slept peacefully that night but as soon as my eyes popped open the next morning, shock hit me again, "ALCOHOL—NONE DETECTED!" Those three words changed everything.

So far, I knew Jack had attended a sorority party Friday night, then walked to a local bar where he supposedly drank too much alcohol. Due to his level of intoxication, another student escorted him to campus and left him less than a block away from the stairwell where he supposedly walked to the bottom, passed out, and choked to death on his own vomit. His body was found five days later. Now if you take alcohol out of the equation, what's left?

No one can dispute the fact that Jack was not intoxicated when he died, no matter what anyone said or did from that point on. Which means you have to throw the Indiana County Coroner's scenario out the window. If Jack was not intoxicated, he couldn't be lying anywhere unconscious due to alcohol consumption. Where's the proof?

So, why was he unconscious? Maybe he wasn't, and if he wasn't, then how did he choke to death on his own vomit? The theory made no sense without alcohol in his blood. Keep in mind: Coroner Streams concluded Jack was intoxicated without any toxicological evidence, the day after his body was found. Three months later, even after the report came back with no alcohol detected in his blood at the time of death, Streams released this statement to the press:

> "The final report also confirmed that alcohol was a contributing factor in this death," Streams said. But he noted, "The exact level of alcohol could not be determined."

Isn't "NONE DETECTED" a level?

I scanned the autopsy report one more time, looking for clues. Maybe I missed something the first hundred times around. No bruises on his body. So, he couldn't have tumbled down all those concrete steps or fallen off the twenty-foot concrete wall. No marks on his body except for a small cut above his left eye. Nothing explained his death.

I knew one thing; this healthy, young male did not just walk down those steps and drop dead in the middle of the night–or at any other time of day. So, how did he die?

At this point, murder sounded like the only real possibility but who wanted this college kid dead, and why? More importantly, why did the coroner keep saying there was alcohol in his body after reading the toxicology report? What was going on?

There was no way around it; I had to talk to the IUP officer who investigated the case. I picked up the phone without hesitation and made an appointment to speak with him the next day. What had he found? What did he think happened to Jack?

John agreed to go, even though he'd be up all night baking bread. He sounded as anxious as I did to hear what the officer had to say about his brother's death. He promised to catch a few hours of sleep before driving us to Indiana for our afternoon appointment. I jotted down a few questions off the top of my head, knowing there'd be a lot more after seeing the IUP police report.

Funny how taking one step forward empowers you to take the next. I picked up the phone and called the Pennsylvania Liquor Control Board (LCB) in Punxsutawney (the little town thirty minutes north of Indiana where the famous groundhog peeks out of his hole on February 2 to see his shadow—or not). One newspaper article mentioned a citation issued to the local bar for serving Jack alcohol, which now sounded bizarre.

I knew absolutely nothing about issued citations, however, the headline *"No appeal granted"* above one article drew my attention. What did that mean? Why did the denied appeal make headlines in this case? Grasping at straws, I asked the state trooper on the phone about the denied appeal.

"The conflict in this case was a dispute about the time and date the LCB learned about the violation and the one-year deadline for filing the charges," the LCB bureau chief said. "There was a difference of opinion but the judge ruled the deadline expired."

"Is this normal procedure?" I said, not knowing what else to ask.

He said he had no idea why the charges were filed four days after the one-year deadline; he didn't work in that office at the time.

"Slipped through a loop-hole, I mean crack, I guess. I think the questions you have will have to be answered by someone higher up," he said, referring me to the LCB attorney who handled the case.

Before he hung up, I asked to speak to the state trooper listed as the investigator in the case, hoping to get a few more answers.

63

Request denied. So, what did I do? Call back on the sly and innocently ask for the state trooper by name. As soon as I started asking a question, the investigating officer switched the call back to the bureau chief without saying a word. Boy, was my face red!

"Do you have more questions?" the chief said sternly.

"No," I said, feeling like the kid caught with my hand stuck in the cookie jar. "I just wanted to thank you for your time."

My confidence hit the ground like a lead balloon. Unnerved, I decided to venture down the path of least resistance. Maybe the girl Jack dated knew something. The former roommate told me her name, and her parents' number was listed in the phone book. They lived in Penn Hills, too—not far from the place where Jack grew up.

The girl's mother rattled off her daughter's phone number at IUP without question then said how sorry she felt for Jack's parents. I thanked her, hung up, and dialed the number. After several rings, her machine picked up, I identified myself and left my number, hoping she'd call back.

That's enough for today, I thought, feeling totally drained. A moan escaped my lips, as the thought of covering a local meeting for the paper that night crossed my mind. Down-shifting out of the major adrenaline rush of investigating a murder all day, back into sitting through another boring council meeting for hours felt unbearable, but the rent had to be paid.

Have you ever attended your local council meeting? You should, at least once in your life. This is the level of government where citizens can voice their opinions and influence lawmakers. Be prepared, however; one item on the agenda can drag on for months.

For instance, installing a stop sign at the corner of whatever streets may spark endless debate. Council members take turns discussing the need for the proposed stop sign, the possibility of the stop sign, and every ramification of placing the proposed stop sign at the suggested location, the cost of erecting the stop sign, and so on for hours. Egos run rampant as each council member vies to keep his or her political image and agenda alive.

When they've finished chewing on a subject for sometimes hours, the issue is then opened to public discussion. Residents step forward to be heard; those directly affected by the stop sign speak their minds as well as a handful of other residents who never miss a meeting and feel it's their civic duty to confront council no matter what the issue. Needless to say, controversy develops and polite verbal battles ensue. Residents go on the attack and politicians, wanting to be seen in the best possible light, talk on and on in an attempt to emerge from the fray smelling as sweet as roses.

Granted, the antics are interesting and amusing at first, but after a few years the thrill is definitely gone. It's amazing anything ever gets done, but eventually it does. School board meetings fare about as well. You learn to sit for hours taking notes, hoping for a good quote or two, while mentally piecing together a story and always anxious about missing your deadline. However, the biggest fear is coming up empty handed and facing a blank page.

"We saved six inches for you," the voice from the copy desk says an hour before deadline. "You have to come up with something." No matter what, the space has to be filled. You might want to keep that in mind the next time you read or watch the news.

Believe me, writing about anything became a real challenge with so many questions rattling around in my brain. My life turned upside-down in one week, notes scattered everywhere!

Notes about notes, strategy diagrams, reference books, slips of paper with phone numbers piled on tables and chairs, covering just about every space on my tiny living room floor.

Looking back, I'm amazed at my fortitude. Nothing stopped me from gathering information, organizing and trying to understand it, then figuring out the next step, which felt as important as the one before. There was no way to accept the fact that someone might get away with murder and these parents might never know the truth.

I guess I took the pledge seriously and believed with my whole heart in the promise of justice for all. Idealistic and naive, perhaps, but then you'd have to say that about everyone who's ever fought and died for human rights.

If no one stands and fights, we all pay a very high price. Every failure to defend individual rights chips away another piece of the foundation on which this country stands.

I thought of Jack's mother often and desperately wanted to tell her the truth about her son, but had to respect John's decision to keep her in the dark. He didn't think she could handle dealing with her son's death again and he knew her best. Still, I knew we'd have to meet one day out of sheer necessity.

"She must have questions," I thought constantly. Did she believe her son died the way they said he did? Did she ever wonder if he was murdered? Could she even go there? I couldn't imagine what went through her mind on a daily basis, but the fact remained, she had answers no one else possessed.

What did she see and hear the night her son's body was found in the stairwell? What did her son talk to her about days, weeks, months before his death? How did she feel believing that her only child drank himself to death?

These questions weighed on my mind as my fingers typed words into the computer, filling the six-inch space with bland council meeting tidbits for the morning edition. With a touch of a button, the story sped to the copy desk. I jumped in the car and headed home.

The blinking red light on my answering machine beckoned in the dark as I opened the front door of my apartment. Jack's girlfriend called back and invited me to call her anytime. I glanced at the clock—almost midnight. Maybe too late I thought, while pushing the buttons on the phone. She didn't mind and seemed eager to talk.

"I spent Thursday night at Jack's apartment," she said. "Everything seemed normal. He didn't seem upset or talk about anything out of the ordinary. Before I left Friday morning, we planned to meet Saturday night. I was upset when he didn't show for our date, but knew he'd eventually call to explain. No one expected anything was wrong until Jack didn't show up for classes Monday morning."

She told me to call back if I had any more questions. I agreed and extended the same invitation if she remembered anything else she wanted to share. After hanging up, I debated whether to make one more call. I looked up the number earlier that day and had thought about contacting this person all day.

As the phone rang and rang, I jotted down a few questions to ask the person who, according to Jack's former roommate, was the last to see Jack alive. The fact that this person might have been considered a prime suspect had this been a murder case never crossed my mind. Of course, once a death is ruled accidental there are no suspects.

The polite young man who answered the phone never mentioned the time. Instead, he seemed completely at ease and ready to talk about his encounter with Jack that Friday night. He recalled seeing Jack leaning up against the wall in a local bar called Caleco's. He said he didn't know Jack very well and had only seen him a couple of times at fraternity parties where they had exchanged a few words.

"I saw how intoxicated he was so I offered to walk him to the dorm to find him a place to sleep it off," the student said. "Jack was angry and saying he was going to fight the Phi Delts. Outside the bar, people were shouting and there was some kind of scuffle going on. Jack wanted to jump in but I grabbed him by his jacket. The police came and broke it up. We left and walked towards campus. I didn't know where he lived, so I kept asking him but he wouldn't tell me. I went into the dorm to find him a place to sleep it off but when I came out he was gone."

He estimated the time to have been around one-thirty Saturday morning.

"I don't know how they can say Jack died the way he did. I've seen people drunker than he was that night. He wasn't staggering or falling down or anything like that and I can't believe they said he went down into that stairwell to relieve himself. When we were walking back to campus, Jack even stopped to pee right on someone's lawn. He didn't try to hide or anything."

As soon as he heard Jack was missing, the student went to Indiana Borough police to report walking Jack to a dormitory located less than two city blocks from the stairwell. Now the way the coroner had developed his theory made more sense. He really did base his entire scenario on this kid's story.

It was a convenient theory to say the least, very tidy—no foul play—an open and shut case. No publicity. No investigation. A neat little package tied up with a bow, and delivered to the traumatized parents who trusted him. Why not? He was a public official with a title. And who can argue with the facts, especially when it's your son's own fault he's dead.

Would I have done anything different if in their shoes? I'm sure the death or even more unthinkable, the murder, of my own child would push me straight over the edge. My heart ached for these people and we had never met.

Remaining objective grew harder by the minute. This being my first investigation, I wondered how other investigative reporters managed to maintain a delicate balance when faced with incriminating evidence.

Teetering on this fine line turned into a hell of a balancing act as the story developed over time. I stayed centered, pulling myself back from the brink of being emotionally involved by repeating, "There are two sides to every story," several times at night in bed.

I reached for the notebook on my nightstand, jotted down the last note of the day, "Get Indiana Borough police report!" I turned over and nestled my head into my pillow, determined to catch a few winks before heading off with John to meet with the IUP officer in the morning. He had to have read the toxicology report.

What would he say?

# SEVEN

*America isn't easy. America is advanced citizenship. You've got to want it and want it bad. It's going to put up a fight.*

Michael Douglas, Actor,
The American President

John slowed the minivan down to a crawl in order to maneuver the snow-covered, windy roads safely. The trip to Indiana might take a little longer today, but we felt more relaxed on our second trip. We chatted and admired the scenery; John had even brought some special music to accompany us along the way.

"You have to hear this," he said, smiling like the proverbial cat that swallowed the canary. "It's the new Tom Petty and there's one specific song you have to hear." John shoved the cassette into the slot on the dashboard, cranked up the volume then glanced over to catch my reaction. The song entitled, "I Won't Back Down" spoke of taking a stand, facing adversity, and fighting with all your might to the bitter end. Tom Petty and Heartbreakers sounded determined, defiant—more than ready to kick some serious ass—I loved it! Pretty soon we were both singing along, mumbling words we didn't know but didn't care. It was the perfect pep song to energize and inspire us on the way to facing anyone or anything that day and just about every time we headed back to Indiana from then on.

Despite only having slept a few hours, John seemed cheerful, in a good mood. No threats, cussing or red-faced anger as we drove along singing and talking. Saying we were happy sounds funny, considering our mission and anxiety levels—calm on the outside, fight or flight mode on the inside. We didn't talk about the meeting with the IUP officer. The less said the better; I didn't know what might trigger John's rage.

John stands about five-foot-ten and has a stocky, muscular build with almost the same physique as a weight lifter. His visible physical strength coupled with his tough, street-wise voice and manner left no doubt in anyone's mind about messing with this guy. His persona plainly stated, "I'll punch your lights out."

Today, however, his blue eyes twinkled, all smiles. Perhaps the twinkle reflected the shimmer of light he now saw at the end of his nightmarish tunnel. Now he knew for a fact that his little brother did not drink himself to death. He was right.

John looked empowered driving back to the scene of the crime to search for answers to questions that had haunted him constantly over the past two years. I saw a different, gentler side of him that day. I hoped he could maintain his composure in front of the IUP officer.

We were almost there. As soon as we hit the long bridge we crossed the last time, I knew the small town sat up over two more hills and around the bend. I didn't know what to expect, but based on the IUP officer's warnings I figured the information was not going to be handed to us on a silver platter. At least I'd be able to see the police report even if the university refused to release it. Deep breath.

"Well, here goes nothing," I said, stepping out of the van across from the main campus entrance. John's face turned red. "Please John, you have to control yourself. Let me do most of the talking," I said, touching his arm. "Okay?"

He looked straight ahead, nodded. Not another word passed between as we walked briskly, fighting the bitter cold wind with every step as we crossed the vast courtyard towards the university administration building at the opposite end. I loved the look and feel of the campus with its quaint, colonial-style red brick buildings encircling the large courtyard. It reminded me of a scene out of a Norman Rockwell painting with a small, ivy-league, New England-style college set against a picturesque backdrop of rolling hills in a friendly, little country town.

I imagined what it'd be like to be one of the many students racing past us in every direction headed to class. What a life! Attend classes, make friends, study, have fun. You're fresh out of high school, away from parents for the first time, testing your immature wings. Freedom, plans for the future, making your own decisions, taking care of yourself, facing challenges on your own.

Wow! I had never looked at college life in that light. Can you imagine what it's like in the fall when thousands of independence-crazed youngsters descend on a small town like this all at once? University administrations must quiver in their boots knowing that thousands of teenagers are about to arrive. No adult supervision, only a handful of administrators relying on another handful or two of university and borough police to keep them all in line. No easy task to say the least.

Gives you a whole different level of respect for those in charge of safely educating thousands of hormone-raging teenagers still wet behind the ears.

As soon as we walked through the door of the Public Safety office, the IUP officer met us at the front desk, then immediately ushered us into his private office and closed the door. Introductions, hand shakes all around, then down to business.

"I'm just going to read this," he said, starting at the beginning of his report.

We were stunned. I scribbled words as fast as my fingers could move, hoping to catch all the important details, which at this point, sounded like everything he said.

Apparently, Jack had left his house with his fraternal big brother around eight-thirty Friday night to attend a sorority party a few blocks from his apartment. They drove the two blocks and Jack parked his car in a lot next to a pizza shop on Oakland Avenue in front of the sorority house.

Between eleven and eleven-thirty, he left the party and walked to a local bar with a group of his fraternity brothers. Students told police Jack drank a lot at the party and at the bar. He was seen playing a game called "Quarters," which the officer explained is a drinking game that involves dropping a shot of whisky into a glass of beer then drinking it. I was not sure how the quarters come into play, but it wasn't important.

The IUP officer stopped reading again to emphasize Jack's comments while in the bar. Jack kept yelling, "Does anyone care that I have a fucking headache!" Other than seeing his outbursts as strange drunken behavior, the significance was lost on me. Why would Jack be yelling about a headache? And why did the officer look at us and read the words twice?

He also pointed out Jack's involvement in a fight with another student, resulting in Jack being escorted out of the bar. Two students reported seeing him cross the street and enter another bar called Caleco's. I recognized the name as the place where Jack met the kid who last saw him alive.

My eyes never left the officer's face except to make sure the point of my pen hit the paper. I got the feeling he knew more than what was written in his report. Of course, he didn't know how much we knew already, which was perfect.

Conducting an investigation is like playing poker. You keep your cards close to your chest until the other person shows his hand. Listen carefully, evaluate the situation, and wait for the perfect moment to play your hand. Do you ever show all your cards? That depends on how the game proceeds. The other person plays a card, you play a card, and you always keep your trump card for last.

The officer assumed we knew nothing about the toxicology report. When he reached that page in his report, he asked us both to step around to the other side of his desk in order to view the document over his shoulder. He pointed to the amounts of alcohol in the stomach and urine with his pen, drawing decimal points and zeros next to the final results. He twisted the pen, exaggerating the decimal points, as he told us about the special training he had received and that he teaches other officers how to deal with drug- and alcohol-related cases.

"Here's the blood level," he said, pointing to "ND*" in the report. "You'll have to ask someone what this means. Do you have a family doctor?" he asked turning to look at John.

"Ask him to explain the amounts to you," the IUP officer said, looking me straight in the eye. I knew he knew, too.

The meeting ended as soon as he read his synopsis, which basically restated the events leading up to Jack's disappearance and the coroner's theory. He ended his report with the sentence, "This information may be confirmed by the lab reports that are pending through the coroner's office."

There was no mention of the final results, just the referral to the coroner's office. I couldn't help but wonder how this officer, specially trained to deal with alcohol- and drug-related cases, felt when he received a copy of this toxicology report. It had to bother him. The truth staring him in the face as the county coroner announced publicly that this student was intoxicated.

As we thanked him, he told us not to hesitate to call if we had any questions. Deep in my heart, I felt he wanted to say more and often wondered why he didn't come right out and tell us no alcohol had been found in Jack's blood when he died.

"Did you see how nervous he was?" John said the second we stepped out of the building. "Did you see how he loosened his tie and opened the top button of his shirt? He was nervous all right. He even walked over and opened the window for air. It's February for Christ's sake! Were you hot? I wasn't hot!"

No but I had lost the function in my right hand and fingers from writing so fast for hours—and my butt was numb. Talk about intense situations. Never in my wildest dreams did I ever think I'd regret not taking shorthand in high school. Who'd have thought?

We sat back quietly listening to music on the ride back home. Not Tom Petty, but something calm and soothing. I stared out the window replaying the moment the investigating officer drew decimal points on the toxicology report in my mind. He wanted to make sure we understood the amounts of alcohol in the stomach and urine. Why? He did not say a word about the blood except to refer John to a doctor. No place to put decimal points, no numbers, and he never uttered the words, "NONE DETECTED."

I had a lot to think about on the way back. As soon as John turned the minivan into his driveway, I jumped out, waved, hopped into my car and sped away. Twenty minutes to make it home and call the Allegheny County coroner's office before it closed. The roads were clear, ten minutes tops. I had to talk to someone about the decimal points the IUP officer drew on the report.

I ran through the door, grabbed the phone, scattered slips of paper all over the place, found the number, dialed, and held my breath. The phone rang and rang. "Please be open," I prayed out loud. "Come on, pick up the phone." No sleep tonight without answers.

Finally, a woman picked up, listened to my question, then switched me to the Allegheny County Toxicology Lab—a place I didn't even know existed until that moment. If they didn't have answers, who did? The anonymous college term paper scenario worked again. The lab technician listened to the numbers—including decimals—thought for a few seconds, then blew me away.

"Those numbers indicate the possibility of the alcohol being displaced or having gone through the system. Alcohol is usually displaced within twenty-four hours or longer if a person is drinking heavily. Usually, however, blood alcohol increases in a dead body because bacteria start to react in the blood. I can say a person with these readings was not intoxicated when they died. Based on the fermentation process, which naturally occurs in the body after death, you also have to conclude that this person was not dead very long when the body was found. If a body is dead a long time there is always some level of alcohol found in the blood from decomposition."

Well, that sure shoots the hell out of the theory that Jack was in the stairwell for five days! Alcohol found in the stomach and urine but not in the blood. The words, "That's physically impossible!" rang in my ears from a previous conversation with the deputy county coroner in Pittsburgh. I'd had enough for one day; my head was spinning. I needed to grab a bite to eat before heading off to cover a school board meeting for the paper in less than an hour.

There were questions, more questions, and very few answers. My biggest question being, "What the hell is going on?" Everyone claims to have seen Jack "highly intoxicated" the night he disappeared but no alcohol turns up in his blood. He's missing for five days and based on the physical evidence was still alive. Now this gets creepy.

He had to be someplace while alive, which begs the question: how did he end up dead in a stairwell close to the place where the last person claims to have seen him alive five days before his body is found? I know he didn't stand there for five days, walk down into the stairwell and die. Nothing made sense, except now I totally believed Streams really did base his entire theory on the student's statement.

After filing my school board story at the office, I went home and poured over my almost legible notes from the meeting earlier that day. The notes were sketchy at best but there was enough new data to construct a diagram and arrange the events into some kind of logical sequence. I tried hard to make sense of it all but some pieces of this bizarre puzzle did not fit, no matter how many times I switched them around.

I drew many diagrams during this venture to help me sort out details and plan the next move. Of course, most of the time I flew by the seat of my pants. When opportunity knocked, we answered.

Page 1 of toxicology report shows amount of alcohol detected in stomach and urine, decimals and zero penciled in by IUP officer. Blood content ND*

| | | | | ROCHE | ROCHE BIOMEDICAL LABORATORIES, INC. |
|---|---|---|---|---|---|
| SPECIMEN # 3-95-493-0143-1 | TYPE S | PRI/ALT CR | REPORT STATUS FINAL PG 2 | 03 12 | |
| TIME 1015 UB,GASTRIC,2GRAY SEE BELOW 1LIVER,1HEART,1KIDNEY IN-@TISSUE POST MORTEM BLD | | | | CLINICAL INFORMATION | |
| | | | | PHYSICIAN ID GRIFFIN | PATIENT ID |
| PATIENT NAME DAVIS , JACK | | SEX M | AGE (YR/MOS) 020/00 | ACCOUNT INDIANA HOSPITAL LAB. HSSNP 3780321 | |
| PT. ADD | | | | P.O. 78461   01760   04 INDIANA HOSPITAL          04 | |
| DATE OF SPECIMEN 10/22/87 | DATE RECEIVED 10/23/87 | DATE REPORTED 12/29/87 | 0965 | INDIANA , PA  15701- #12-357-7160 PAP | |

| TEST | RESULT | | LIMITS | LAB |
|---|---|---|---|---|
| COCAINE | NT** | | ND | ND |
| BENZOYLECGONINE (MCG/ML) | NT | | 0.1 | 2.6 |
| ECGONINE METYL ESTER (MCG/ML) | NT | | DETECTED & IDENTIFIED | 1.6 |
| THC | NT | | ND | ND |
| 11-NOR-DELTA 9-CARBOXY-THC (NG/ML) | NT | | ND | 23 |

* NONE DETECTED
** NOT TESTED

URINE CHEMISTRY BY DIPSTICK ANALYSIS REVEALED THE PRESENCE OF PROTEINS AND BLOOD; OTHERWISE THE TEST WAS UNREMARKABLE. OTHER THAN THE ABOVE FINDINGS EXAMINATION OF THE SUBMITTED SPECIMENS DID NOT REVEAL ANY POSITIVE DATA OF TOXICOLOGICAL SIGNIFICANCE BY PROCEDURES OUTLINED IN THE ACCOMPANYING ANALYSIS SUMMARY SHEET.

COMMENTS AND CONCLUSIONS:
1. THE EXCITANT-STIMULANT COCAINE IS A SCHEDULE II LISTED DEA CONTROLLED SUBSTANCE. ECGONINE METHYL ESTER IS A METABOLITE OF COCAINE AND IS INDICATIVE OF COCAINE USE. BENZOYLECGONINE IS A BIOTRANSFORMATION PRODUCT OF COCAINE THAT MAY OCCUR OUTSIDE THE BODY. THE MANIFESTATION OF COCAINE INCLUDE RESTLESSNESS, EXCITEMENT, AND GARRULOUSNESS.
2. THE PRESENCE OF THE METABOLITES, ECGONINE METHYL ESTER AND BENZOYL-ECGONINE, IN THE BLOOD OF THE DECEDENT WITHOUT THE PARENT COMPOUND MAKE IT DIFFICULT TO ACCURATELY DEFINE THE INFLUENCE OF THE SUBSTANCE ON THIS INDIVIDUAL.

RESULTS ARE FLAGGED IN ACCORDANCE WITH AGE DEPENDENT REFERENCE RANGES          REPC

Page 2 of Toxicology report shows ND* stands for
NONE DETECTED.

|  |  |  |  |  |  |  |  |
|---|---|---|---|---|---|---|---|
| SPECIMEN # | TYPE | PRIMAR | REPORT STATUS |  |  | ROCHE | ROCHE BIOMEDICAL LABORATORIES, INC. |
| 035-188-0143-1 | S | CB | FINAL | PG 3 | 03 C |  |  |
| ADDITIONAL INFORMATION | | | | | CLINICAL INFORMATION | | |
| TIME 1015 UB,GASTRIC,2GRAY SEE BELOW 1LIVER,1HEART,1KIDNEY IN-@TISSUE POST MORTEM BLD | | | | | PHYSICIAN ID  GRIFFIN | | PATIENT ID |
| PATIENT NAME | | | SEX | AGE (YRS/MOS) | ACCOUNT | | |
| DAVIS , JACK | | | M | 020/00 | INDIANA HOSPITAL LAB. HSSWP P.O. 78461                 01760 INDIANA HOSPITAL                           04 INDIANA         , PA 15701-    04 | | 3780821 |
| PT. ADD. | | | | | | | |
| DATE OF SPECIMEN | DATE RECEIVED | DATE REPORTED | | | | | |
| 10/22/87 | 10/23/87 | 12/23/87 | 0945 | | 812-357-7160         PAP | | |
| TEST | | | RESULT | | | LIMITS | LAB |

LEE M. BLUM, PH.D.
TOXICOLOGIST
ANALYSIS SUMMARY

1. DIFFERENCE SPECTROPHOTOMETRY FOR:
   CARBOXYHEMOGLOBIN, SULFHEMOGLOBIN

2. HEADSPACE GAS CHROMATOGRAPHY FOR:
   VOLATILE INTOXICANTS AND INHALANTS WITH BOILING POINTS UP TO 180 C.:
   ALCOHOLS, ACETONE, ACETALDEHYDE, HYDROCARBON SOLVENTS AND FUELS,
   ESTER-, ETHER-, AND KETONE SNIFFING SOLVENTS, FREONS, CHLORINATED
   SOLVENTS, VOLATILE ORGANIC ANESTHETICS.

3. DIRECT/INDIRECT COLOR AND FLUORESCENT TESTS FOR:
   ACETAMINOPHEN, BROMIDES, CYANIDE, ETHCHLORVYNOL, SALICYLATES,
   TRIHALOALIPHATICS.

4. IMMUNOCHEMICAL ASSAYS FOR:
   BENZODIAZEPINES, BENZOYLECGONINE (COCAINE), CANNABINOIDS (MARIHUANA),
   OPIATES, PHENCYCLIDINE (PCP).

5. THIN-LAYER AND GAS CHROMATOGRAPHY OF EXTRACTS FOR:
   ANTICONVULSANTS, ANTIDEPRESSANTS, ANTIHISTAMINES, BENZODIAZEPINES,
   CAFFEINE, CARDIOREGULATORIES, SEDATIVE-HYPNOTICS, COCAINE AND AMPHETAM
   TYPE STIMULANTS, HALLUCINOGENS, NICOTINE, QUININE/QUINIDINE, STRICHNOE
   ALKALOIDS, NARCOTIC ANALGESICS (EXCEPT MORPHINE).

6. GAS CHROMATOGRAPHY/MASS SPECTROMETRY FOR:

RESULTS ARE FLAGGED IN ACCORDANCE WITH AGE DEPENDENT REFERENCE RANGES        REPC

Page 3 of Toxicology report showing analysis of tests performed, some checking for "sudden death."

# EIGHT

*I'm here to fight for truth, justice and the American way.*

Superman

Parts of this story are hard to relive again. I've told it so many times to so many people over the years and the amazing part is the memories still hurt. I woke up this morning with exactly the same tight ball of anxiety mixed with fear sitting in the pit of my stomach that I did the day after our meeting with the IUP officer. The diagram drawn the night before led straight to the horrific story I must relive on these pages today.

I called John around noon to ask about Jack's personal belongings. More specifically, I wanted to see his notebooks from his last semester. He died in October, two months into his sophomore year. Maybe he scribbled something down that might shed light on what was going on in his life at the time.

"I don't know who has that stuff and we can't ask Elaine or Jack's father. I still don't want them to know anything about what we are doing," John said. "I think I saw some of his stuff somewhere. Let me look around and see what I can find."

I promised to respect John's request for secrecy when we joined forces but now felt his caution held us back. Jack's parents had to be told sooner or later. They were there the night their son's body was found in the stairwell and must have their own perspective on what happened. For now, however, I'd have to bide my time.

Besides writing advertising copy for the *Tribune* that day, I planned to place a few phone calls from the list I had put together the night before. The mere thought of writing ad copy felt impossible at the time. There was nothing like driving miles to some flower shop or restaurant to take pictures, then write some stupid story to convince people to buy something in the midst of a murder investigation!

Freelance writers only get paid after their stories are printed, or as they say, upon publication. Which means the only way to survive is to create regular daily, weekly, and monthly assignments such as writing ad copy to earn an almost-steady paycheck.

Looking back, I don't know how I managed to stay afloat with all the financial and emotional chaos in my personal life back then. My children and I struggled to keep our sense of family intact and find some solid ground to stand on. After a nasty divorce, I had nothing—absolutely nothing. I escaped the abusive eighteen-year marriage with a card table, a twin-size mattress, my clothes, and a few personal items.

My eldest son already lived in a third-floor apartment in my mother's house. My daughter and youngest son decided to stay with their father after seeing my bare one-bedroom apartment. I told myself I'd probably make the same choice in their shoes. Still, it felt as if someone ripped my heart out of my chest. These were tough times indeed and struggling to scrape together rent became my biggest challenge every month.

So you see, talking about those not-so-good old days is not easy. When you mix the personal chaos in my life together with the confusion in this case, you come up with an overwhelming and seemingly endless drama.

An unbelievable drama that unfolded right in front my eyes on a daily basis and at a moment's notice. I was in the middle of a conversation with Indiana Borough Police Chief Anthony Antolik when John knocked on the door around noon with Jack's fraternity pledge book plus a few other personal items he'd found in his house.

"Would you like to come to the station to discuss the report?" Antolik said, while I silently waved John through the front door. "Hold on a minute," I said, holding my hand over the receiver to ask John.

"Yes!" he said, moving his lips without sound while nodding his head.

Within minutes, we were on the road back to Indiana. No music playing or singing this time. We were both too anxious to do anything but pull our thoughts together. Two meetings with two police officers to discuss two different police reports in two days set my teeth on edge. I bounced along as John drove, trying to jot down intelligent questions as well as prepare John for the unexpected meeting at the same time.

The tone of his voice as he drove along coupled with the defiant cock of his head as he spoke signaled the need to diffuse his anger before we got to the police station. His driving matched his mood. He scared the hell out of me a couple times taking a few curves almost on two wheels. I still can see his red face as we jumped out of the van and raced across the street against the bitter cold winter wind to make our appointment on time.

"I just want to remind you that we only dealt with this case until the body was found," Antolik said, sitting down behind his big wooden desk and plopping a yellow folder down in front of him. "When his body was found on campus, the case fell under the university's jurisdiction. We only dealt with the missing person report his roommates filed."

He retold most of what we had heard the day before from the IUP officer, with a few exceptions. His report included more details and names of people contacted during the search for Jack, the missing person. They interviewed several sorority and fraternity members. Antolik also requested hand-written statements from the same student I talked to who claimed to be the last to have seen Jack alive, as well as separate statements from each of the two female students with whom Jack had hooked up while walking across the street to Caleco's, the second bar he visited that night.

Unlike the IUP officer, Antolik didn't read the entire report to us. Instead, he offered an overview of actions taken and the results of his investigation. He restated his theory about Jack being abducted, exactly as printed in the newspaper. He talked about the sorority party Jack attended that Friday night and how the girls refused to talk without an attorney present.

"They were worried about getting in trouble because of alcohol at the party," he said, reaching inside his folder for a large, brown envelope. "Have you seen the pictures yet? I have the autopsy photos and some others if you want to see them."

I stopped breathing, my eyes as wide as saucers. Pictures? There were pictures? Oh, my God! I never considered pictures and now had only seconds to weigh my options. No, I didn't want to see them—who does? I had to look. I knew I had to look. "This might be my only chance," I thought, swallowing a big gulp of air.

"Yes, I want to see them," I said, holding out my shaking hand. John said nothing.

Antolik handed me the stack of black-and-white eight-by-tens, I turned sideways in the chair facing John on my right. He'd only be able to see the blank white back of each photo, which, of course, did not shield his eyes from the look of horror on my face. I'd seen pictures of Jack before. In one he's Uncle Jack, smiling as he holds John's infant daughter for the first time; in another he's a high school senior posing for his yearbook portrait—the same photo used in most newspaper articles.

This time his face was a bloody mess. His crumbled body looked strangely contorted, his head jammed against the red brick wall of the science building in the bottom in the stairwell. Streams of dark blood covered the lower half of his face. Not at all what I had expected to see.

Where did all the blood come from if he choked to death on his own vomit? I didn't know how to react. He looked like someone beat the hell out of him! I struggled to remain calm, fidgeting in the now very uncomfortable, big wooden chair. Several glossy photos showed his body from different angles in the stairwell; others showed his body lying on a steel slab in the autopsy room. I'd never seen anything like this—not even in nursing school or while working in a hospital.

In some of the photos he was still dressed in the clothes he wore when he left his apartment the Friday night he disappeared. It was strange; his arms and legs were sticking up in mid-air like they were stiff. Others showed his young naked body stretched out on the shiny table with his chest carved open like a gutted fish. There was a large, deep, empty, dark hole from his neck to below his navel. In contrast, his childlike face looked as if he slept peacefully in the middle of a pleasant dream, without blood on his face.

"I want to see them," John said, looking me straight in the eye.

"Please don't look, John," I pleaded. "You don't want to remember your brother this way."

He snatched the photos out of my hands, his face already bright red from the neck up. I stared at the floor, waiting for the explosion. Every once in a while I'd glance up. Antolik met my eyes. The room was silent except for the sound of me sniffling back the tears stinging in my eyes. John stared at each picture for what seemed like forever without saying a word. He didn't need to; his small frequent gasps for air said it all.

"I want a copy of that report," John said, slapping the pile of photos onto the desk.

"You'll have to get a subpoena," Antolik said, gathering the scattered photos in his hands and tapping them on the desk to create a neat pile. John stormed out the door. I jumped up right behind him, stopped quickly to thank the officer for his time, and then ran to keep up. John stomped fast and furious out of the building, down the steps, and across the street to the parking lot. He stopped on a dime in front of me. We almost collided. Then he turned to face me with tears pooled in both eyes.

"Fry 'em!" John yelled. "Fry them all! Those dirty bastards! Did you see all the blood on his face? Why is there blood on his face? His nose was broken; that's why! I'm telling you his nose was broken! It was swollen. I know my brother and no one can tell me his nose isn't broken! Didn't you see it! His nose was broken!"

"I couldn't tell, John. You know your brother's face better than I do," I said calmly. "That would explain all the blood, though."

Uncle Jack holding his new born niece.
(Photograph compliments of Elaine Davis Lynch)

Jack opening birthday presents.
(Photograph compliments of Elaine Davis Lynch)

"I'll get a goddamn subpoena!" John ranted as he turned the key in the door of the van. "Get a subpoena, my ass! Bastard! My brother was beaten to death! No one is going to tell me he wasn't! Fucking assholes! Fry 'em all!"

My heart pounded as John slammed the gearshift into reverse, jolting us backwards out of the parking space. Another quick slam into drive, and we sped away. I felt so bad for him. Looking at those pictures hurt me; I couldn't even imagine how I'd feel if that was my brother in the pictures.

We barely exchanged two words on the way home. There was nothing left to say. I stared out the window, not noticing any of the snow-covered trees whizzing by. Jack's bloody face was all I saw. Every once in a while I'd glance over at John to see how he was doing. He didn't have to say anything; I knew what he was thinking.

My insides shook as I sat on my couch that night, the shocking pictures still fresh in my mind. Not even my favorite television show could shut out the gruesome images I had witnessed that day. I felt numb, scared, terrified, stunned and very alone. I crawled into bed, pulled the covers over my head and tried to replace the living nightmare in my mind, then panicked. I gulped one rapid deep breath after another hoping to calm my fears and fall asleep—or at least knock myself out!

This might sound crazy, but that's the first night I saw Jack next to my bed. I felt his presence, saw him, his bloody face and twisted body so real. From then on, as soon as I turned out the light, he was lying there in the same position as in the stairwell. Only difference, he was not dead.

# NINE

*The administration of justice is the firmest pillar of government.*

GEORGE WASHINGTON

If not obsessed with this case before, I was now. My living room and dining room looked like reams of white and yellow paper exploded all over the place. Of course, I told myself I knew what information each pile contained, and what pieces of this bizarre puzzle were missing. I went to bed scared and often wondering what to do next; much to my surprise, I woke up with answers most mornings.

I recently watched a popular one-hour dramatic television show called *Medium*. The program is based on a woman who is contacted by the dead to help resolve their unfinished business before walking into the light. After I saw it, I wondered if that's what had happened to me. I swear I saw and felt Jack next to my bed at night during most of the investigation. I know how crazy that sounds but when you consider the facts in this case, he had good reasons to want his family to know the truth about his death. Perhaps he did use me.

Even as I write now about this incredible experience, I am amazed at the amount of adrenalin surging through my body. Details of this investigation are as fresh in my mind as they were the day they happened. I didn't sleep well last night; parts of this story I'd sooner forget still bother me. Everyone says writing it all out helps purge thoughts from your brain. Well, I've already learned nothing will ever let me forget the details of his case—not even justice.

Believe me, if you've ever seen or been personally acquainted with a murder victim, you never ever forget. The thought of one person violently taking another person's life, especially someone so young, is etched in your heart and soul forever. I still have a hard time believing what happened to this college student and his family. That's why I'm choosing to send this story out into the world, with hopes that maybe someday someone with a conscience, guilty or not, reads it, feels enough compassion in his or her heart to tell the truth and set this family free.

Looking back, I expected this incredible journey to be painful and difficult but now realize the benefits outweigh the costs. As I write each page my spirit grows lighter and there's so much more to tell. Amazing how the passage of time changes your perspective; the first time around the case shocked the hell out of me; today the experience strikes me as unbelievable.

Too bad one of us didn't count how many times we made the 120-mile round trip to Indiana. I'm guessing at least a hundred—or maybe it just felt that way. John and I spent many days doing research in the university library. Newspaper articles helped me piece together an overview of what was going on at the university and around the small town at the time of Jack's death.

The university's football team made the state conference playoffs, thrusting the university into the national spotlight that year. IUP also made headlines for raising over $4.2 million—almost double their projected figures for 1987. To celebrate, a "dinner-dance" complete with "tuxedos, evening gowns, trumpet salutes and popping champagne corks" for over 200 university and campaign officials was held on October 30.

"The jury isn't out anymore," the IUP capital campaign chairman told guests and reporters during the gala event. "The jury is in. IUP is a leader among universities in this state and all of you have shown that you will support our plans to keep it that way."

"Must have been pretty inconvenient to find a dead body, literally, on your doorstep a week before your big party," I said, showing John the article about the fund-raising event as we sat side by side in the library searching back issues of the *Indiana Gazette*, the *Pittsburgh Press*, the *Pittsburgh Post Gazette*, and IUP's student paper, *The Penn*.

That day we also learned that the Indiana County district attorney issued fifty-seven warrants and arrested forty-five "street level" drug dealers in "one of the largest drug busts in Indiana County history" on October 6. Two weeks before Jack's death.

"Look," said John, pointing at an article in the *Indiana Gazette*. "There *was* a fight between fraternities that night. I told you!"

Unlike previous articles, this one called the confrontation a major fraternity fight instead of a "shouting match." Police were called to disperse the crowd and arrests were made due to the damage caused by thrown bricks. We also found two more reported fights, which meant three known fraternity fights occurred the Friday night Jack disappeared.

Was he hauled off in a police car? Is that where he was for five days—in jail? At this point, anything seemed possible. He had to be somewhere.

The last clipping we copied before calling it a day quoted Streams announcing the toxicology report verifies that Jack was "highly intoxicated at the time of his death; although the exact amount of alcohol could not be determined."

Why did he change the words "None Detected" to "Not Determined?" I wondered. His statement made it sound like there was so much alcohol in his body the exact amount could not be determined.

"How about zero, asshole!" John said as we crossed campus back to the van. "They just out and out lied."

I half listened as my mind focused on the bigger picture uncovered that day. The university had held an open house that drew "students from afar" on October 26, five days after Jack's body was found on campus. IUP also launched a major advertising campaign that year, placing full-page ads in *Time* and *Newsweek* magazines.

The date of the university's fund-raising dinner also rang a bell; for some reason the date stuck in my mind. If I remembered correctly, the IUP officer said the university ended its "fact-finding mission" into Jack's death on October 30, the same day as the dinner. No way to be absolutely sure without a copy of the IUP police report.

"Pull over!" I shouted as we headed out of Indiana that day.

"Right here?" John said, visibly shaken. "What's wrong?"

"I'm going to write a letter requesting IUP release its police report. You're going to sign it then go back and give it to the Public Safety director."

"Right now?" John said.

"Right now," I said, scribbling words on a piece of paper then ripping it out of my spiral-bound tablet. John signed it, ripped edge and all, turned the van around, pulled into the IUP police parking lot and together we walked into the IUP Public Safety building. He went up to the receptionist desk, asked to see the Public Safety director, followed her to his office, explained his request and handed him the note.

"I'll pass it on," the man sitting behind the desk said. John thanked him and we left.

"We did it!" I yelled after both van doors slammed shut. "All they can say is no, right?"

Our trip ended on a high note that kept me going the rest of the night. The IUP officer told us during our meeting that the IUP Public Safety director in 1987 had resigned. I needed to talk to him, which meant calling the receptionist we had just met in the Public Safety office and hope she'd be cooperative, which she was.

Turned out, he now lived in Virginia and taught at Radford College. She said he had left his post in February but formally resigned in April 1988. I called directory assistance and got his number.

I could hardly wait to talk to him, but would he talk to me? Why did he leave? What did he think of this case? Did he talk over the results of the toxicology report with his investigating officer? They had to discuss the results at some point; what did they say to each other? If they both knew the truth and didn't say anything, did they obstruct justice? Why didn't anyone say anything? They were not the only police officers to receive a copy of the toxicology report; the Indiana Borough police got one, too.

The picture painted by the facts did not look pretty. A student is murdered, everyone sees the truth in black and white but no one speaks up. Makes you wonder, why?

During the course of this investigation I found an article in the *Pittsburgh Post Gazette* about the parents of a student who was raped and murdered in her dormitory room at Lehigh University on April 15, 1986. The couple wanted a law enacted that would require universities and colleges to "publish an annual brochure with figures on homicide, assault, rape, robbery and burglary on campus" along with other security measures.

"One of the best-kept secrets in the commonwealth, indeed in the nation, is the crime statistics and security measures at our colleges and universities," said Pennsylvania State Representative Richard A. McClatchy, Jr. who introduced the bill into the state legislature in 1987.

Late that afternoon, I picked up the phone and dialed both numbers listed for the former IUP Public Safety director in Virginia. No answer. I didn't leave a message. I tried reaching, Antolik at the Indiana Borough police station, not in either. The state LCB bureau chief was in so I asked him how to get a copy of the citation filed against the bar for serving alcohol to a minor.

"I'll have to check with officials before giving out any information on this case," the state trooper said. "If you have any questions about testimony, call the magistrate's office in Indiana."

"You're welcome to come in and look up the case on the docket files," a woman in the magistrate's office said, then recited their hours of operation.

The next morning, John and I headed straight for the magistrate's office located behind the Indiana County courthouse. I looked up the case number, requested a copy of the only file listed that involved the accused bartender. The clerk took my written request and said she'd be back in a minute. As we stood waiting behind the wooden counter, a large man dressed in a long, black robe rushed up and stood directly in front of us on the other side.

"Are you looking into this case?" he said searching John's eyes first then mine.

"Yes," I said, introducing John as Jack's brother.

"It's about time someone looked into this!" Magistrate Richard Orendorff said, walking across the room in a huff toward a file cabinet. "Give them anything they want," he said loudly to his clerk. "Keep a copy for me in case I'm subpoenaed. This whole thing was a bunch of sour grapes!" He didn't care who heard him. We stared, speechless.

The clerk handed us records pertaining to the case against the bartender. We already knew from newspaper articles the charges were dismissed. There were no files related to the bar. "That case was handled by the state," the clerk said. I looked at her confused. Why did the LCB bureau chief, who works for the state, refer us to the local magistrate? Following the magistrate's exuberant performance, I didn't know what to think.

"Can you believe it!" John said, calmly and quietly as he turned the key in the ignition. "He said it was a bunch of sour grapes. Don't tell me he doesn't know what's going on—he knows what's going on."

I looked through the file on the way home; most of the notes the magistrate had jotted down during the bartender's hearing looked like chicken scratch. I stuck the papers in a folder then sat back and relaxed, admiring the scenery as the van wound up, down and around the now very familiar country roads back to Pittsburgh.

I felt different, and from the content look on John's face, he did, too. A person in a powerful position had confirmed John's long-held suspicions in a few simple words, "This whole thing was a bunch of sour grapes!"

That night, I called a few phone numbers John found scribbled on pieces of paper among Jack's personal items. One belonged to a high school friend who had known Jack for years.

"I was part of the search party but I don't know exactly who found his body that night. I lived with Jack while he was hazing for the fraternity." he said, "We grew apart as soon as he became a member."

I asked him about the night Jack disappeared.

"There were a lot of fights that night," he said. "I think one of them was between Jack's fraternity and the Phi Delts over in fraternity row; that's what they call Seventh Avenue."

He also said it surprised him to hear Jack could get into Al Patti's bar that night.

"Did Jack have someone's I.D.? They usually card right at the door," he said. "Of course, you can get in if you know someone. Maybe he knew someone at the door."

The possibility had never crossed my mind. Did Jack have a fake I.D.? Interesting, especially if he was arrested that night. His real name would not appear in any police logs. Was he arrested for disorderly conduct during one of the several fraternity fights that night?

My thoughts took off in several weird directions once the possibility of a fake I.D. came into play. Anything's possible when all you have to go on is a dead body, strange circumstances, and now "a bunch of sour grapes."

Of course, if you have this case all figured out at this point, please give me a call.

# TEN

*If you see a good fight–get in it!*
                                    Martin Luther King Jr.

The time had come to make an appointment with the editor of the *Tribune-Review* to discuss the story. He remembered the kid in the stairwell then asked what information I had so far before agreeing to meet. I drove the forty-five miles to the main office in Greensburg in record time.

We discussed the toxicology report, the state filing charges against the bar four days late as well as the magistrate's comments. I rattled on for some time, pulling out documents to verify claims and diagrams drawn to explain parts of the case in the most concise manner possible.

At some point—I'm not sure of the exact moment—the magnitude of this story hit me. This might turn out to be a really big scoop! Do newspaper people still use that expression? I was pumped! I guess that's why his lukewarm response confused me. I left our meeting doubting the evidence and myself. Even though he told me to pick a staff reporter to work with, for some reason I got the impression that he didn't believe me.

I drove home deflated. Looking back now, however, I totally understand his reaction. Here comes a freelance reporter. Sure, she's worked for your company for six years, but she's talking murder. It was his job to be skeptical. I, on the other hand, expected him to be blown away and shocked by the toxicology report and he barely batted an eye.

How could I be so wrong? Dreams of publishing a story vanished. Maybe I needed more, I thought, picking up the phone to call Magistrate Orendorff because, quite frankly, I couldn't make heads or tails out of his hearing notes. He explained he only jots down certain details during any hearing because the proceedings are recorded. There was no tape available for this hearing.

"I'm surprised no one has looked into this before now," he said. "I'm not blaming IUP. That's what's going on up here, drinking. But there was something sour in this case. It just wasn't right."

I asked about the case against the bar.

"You'll have to ask the LCB for those records. If they refuse, tell them you're going to the state attorney general to get them," Magistrate Orendorff said in a tone of voice that meant business. "Ask them why four days lapsed. Do your own investigation."

What just happened? Did the magistrate of this little town just tell me something is rotten in Denmark and to find out for myself?

I picked up the phone to ask the state LCB bureau chief for the third time about getting a copy of the citation filed against the bar. Still not able to release it, he again suggested I talk to the LCB attorney who handled the case for the state, then rattled off his phone number.

Within minutes, the attorney was on the line, and much to my surprise, he too recalled the case instantly.

"There was no basis for an appeal of the citation. There was nothing we could do; it was a legal thing," he said. "The citation against the bar was filed past the deadline. The judge had two dates to choose from. He could have picked the earlier date. I tried to make that a point but the judge refused. That should have been enough to keep the case open."

He called the whole thing "a sham."

"No one would come forward. There was no cooperation from the fraternity brothers, like they were trying to protect the bar or something. Finally, the LCB finds this one kid to testify and then they trick him. One girl who was subpoenaed didn't even show up!"

He got it all off his chest.

"How they didn't find his body for five days is beyond me," the LCB attorney said. "I went to college and they checked every door every day. You'd think his frat brothers would show more loyalty to the body of a dead friend than a bar."

"What do you mean?" I said.

"They brought in a fake bartender at the hearing and the LCB had enough to go on in this case before November 17 when they filed the citation four days past the deadline," he said. "The case was thrown out on a legality. I have never seen a case like this where no one would talk. There were at least twenty students who said they saw this kid drinking in a bar that night, but only one would testify."

He talked fast, leaving no room for questions–and I had plenty—but our conversation ended abruptly; he had appointments.

Were the doors on campus checked daily? What's this about a fake bartender? Who brought a fake bartender into court and why? What the hell went on back then?

# ELEVEN

*There is a higher court of justice and that is the court of conscience. It supersedes all the other courts.*

MOHANDAS GANDHI

Falling asleep turned into a nightly challenge as the investigation grew. Taking one deep breath after another was the only way to push facts and figures—as well as the image of Jack's crumbled, bloody body lying on the floor next to my bed—out of my mind. Breathe. Breathe. Sometimes it worked, sometimes the anxiety lasted until the pink shimmering light of dawn peeked around the edge of my window shade.

Overwhelming says it all. I desperately needed to talk with someone about all this stuff. That morning I called a local television station to see what kind of reaction I'd get. The constant pressure and anxiety made me feel like a volcano ready to erupt! The news production manager at a local station, agreed to meet in two days. Perfect. That gave me time to find a way to present the information in a sane, professional manner. I needed help. My body grew weary from hanging out on this limb alone for so long.

As an added bonus, the upcoming meeting with the television news producer pushed me back into high gear. I picked up the phone and made an appointment to speak with Coroner Streams. He suggested that afternoon, I agreed. Time to get some answers straight from the horse's mouth.

Fortunately John could make it. I was going either way. He jumped into the minivan with a full head of steam, ready to confront the coroner but not too happy with the prospect of sitting in the library to do more research.

"All I can say is fry them all!" he said, his face bright red. Once again he retold his fantasy of driving to Indiana with some buddies and a gun, then taking the key players in this unfolding drama into the woods to get answers.

"They'll talk then! You better believe it!"

His frustration matched my own, only he had no problem letting it out.

"I just want the truth," he said that day and forever more.

I totally understood.

As we talked about meeting with Coroner Streams, he quieted down but his face stayed red. Once again we agreed that I'd do the talking. He just had to listen and remain calm—no matter what anyone said or did.

We pulled into the driveway next to the building of the ambulance service Coroner Streams operated a little before two. He introduced himself then showed us two folding chairs near his desk inside the garage. I took the seat to his right, next to the desk; John pulled his chair up between us but further back.

"Do you mind if I record our conversation," I said, placing my small tape deck on the desk in front of him. Streams yelled to his secretary sitting on the other side of the garage to turn the radio down, and we got started.

My plan was simple: act stupid. I found this to be the best way to lower someone's defenses immediately. When the other person feels confident he or she will tell you what you want to know in a pleasant, helpful manner. If you start accusing or demanding, defense mechanisms kick in and you get nowhere. All you have to do is ask a few questions and let the other person do the talking.

"I based my original theory on the statement made by the last person who saw Jack alive and the autopsy findings," Streams said, scanning the autopsy report.

"Can you explain the toxicology report to us," I said, acting as if it was Greek to me. Happy to oblige, he took the document out of his file and flipped through the pages.

"A lot of alcohol found in his stomach and some found in his urine," the coroner said. "None detected in his blood because it could not be tested. As you know, his body was not found for five days and was decomposed. The blood was in a gel state, like rotten, so it could not be tested."

What'd he say? Huh? My face must have at least shown an element of surprise and confusion but I just nodded and acted like his words made everything crystal clear. What was clear was that Streams didn't know what he was talking about. Jack's body was not decomposed and the blood was tested. The fact that the county coroner did not have to have a medical license amazed me. He is the person who determines how and when someone died, whether the death was accidental or involved foul play. So, how can a person with no medical, forensic or scientific background competently perform this very important job?

John sat quietly absorbing every word. He grabbed the back of his neck and twisted his head from side-to-side a few times to release tension.

"There's one more thing I don't understand," I said, reaching for the toxicology report in the coroner's hand. "Down here at the bottom of the page under alcohol it states 'ND*' or 'None

Detected' in his blood. It doesn't say not tested. I've talked to the people at Roche Laboratories, who conducted the test. They assured me that if the blood was not tested, it would state in the report the blood could not be tested. Which means the lab performed the test and no alcohol was found in his blood at the time of death."

Streams flipped nervously back and forth through the pages of the toxicology report a few times. "They could not determine the amount," he said. "I remember something about that when I got this report back."

"I've also talked to the Allegheny County coroner's office and they said if no alcohol was detected in this blood at the time of death, this person could not have been intoxicated when he died."

"That's just not true," he said, shaking his head with a slight grin on his face as if I'd been misinformed. "Maybe we better talk to Dr. Griffin. He is the one who explained this to me and I'm sure he can explain it better to both of you than I can."

Within minutes, Coroner Streams had Dr. Griffin on the line, switched the call over to speaker so we could hear the conversation, and repeated what I had said about the alcohol.

"That's just not true," Dr. Griffin said. "What happened in this case is the alcohol metabolized out of his body after he was dead. If I remember correctly, he was dead for five days before the body was found."

When he started explaining how red blood cells continue to function after death my eyes almost popped out of my head! He told us to call his office and set up an appointment to meet with him in person, and we thanked him. Streams stood up, shook our hands, and showed us to the door.

"Did you see his face when you told him what the Allegheny County coroner's office said about the report," John said as soon as we sat down in the van. "His face was as red as his necktie. He didn't know what to say."

Which was true. Streams repeated what the pathologist told him. I am not a medical doctor or pathologist either but I knew one thing for certain—a dead body does not metabolize anything after death. Dead is dead. The body ceases to function—period! How could this medical doctor say these things? Was I wrong? He is the doctor, after all.

Dr. Griffin's words echoed in my ears, "Rotten blood...the alcohol was absorbed and processed by the body after death."

"Did we just enter the *Twilight Zone* or did things just work differently in Indiana?" I wondered as John quietly drove us home.

I had just enough time to contact the IUP Public Safety office to check on the status of John's request. "I have no idea when or if the request will be granted," the director said. "It's in the administration's hands now and there is nothing I can do at this point. As soon as I hear anything I'll let you know."

Details of the interview with Coroner Streams replayed in my head the rest of the night. I was still stunned. Did this medical doctor/pathologist, who advises the coroner in this county, believe a body continues to function after death?

That evening while walking through the mall half-heartedly looking for something professional to wear to the television station in the morning, the doctor's words kept running through my head. How could he say such a thing? Could he be right? My sister thought a navy blue suit best but in my state of mind, I settled on the first black suit off the rack that fit. I wasn't presenting my case in court—just to a local news station.

The meeting started in the lobby then moved to inner offices as soon as the producer heard a few details. He instantly recalled the kid whose body was found in the stairwell at IUP. The toxicology report results grabbed his attention immediately.

"We do a lot of work with Dr. Cyril Wecht," he said. "Do you mind if I make a copy of this report and let him look at it? I'd like to get his opinion."

Gravity was the only thing holding my feet on the floor. Did I mind? Did I mind? Are you kidding! Finally, an expert—a world-renowned expert, to say the least—would evaluate the report. I wanted to dance for joy! This was it, he'd either confirm my findings or not. If he did, we'd be playing in a whole different ball game. Hell, a whole different league!

Waiting turned into pure hell and I questioned myself daily. What if I was wrong? Maybe I misinterpreted the results and would end up looking like a fool. Deep down inside, though, I knew the truth. I just knew it. A smile spread across my face every time the fact that—THE—Dr. Cyril Wecht was looking at my case hit me. I pinched myself and had a few friends pinch me, too.

Dr. Wecht investigated famous cases, such as President John F. Kennedy's assassination, Elvis Presley's and Marilyn Monroe's untimely deaths, as well as high profile cases all over the world. If he agreed with my findings, what else did I need? He'd get the public attention this family needed to find the truth.

At this point, all I could do was wait for his opinion and university officials to decide whether to release their police report. I needed a rest and money. Things were stressful on the financial front. I spent every waking moment thinking about my next move, evidence collected and needed. I borrowed money to pay the rent. No turning back. I still completed assignments for the paper, mostly at night, which left me free to pursue new leads at the drop of a hat during the day.

"Do you have a copy of the addendum to the autopsy report?" the television news producer said on the phone a few days after our meeting.

"I don't know?" I said, embarrassed. "What is it?"

"It's the conclusion the pathologist made after receiving the toxicology results from the coroner," he said. "It should be attached to the autopsy report. If you don't have it, call the coroner. He has to have the addendum."

Coroner Streams had a copy and invited me to pick it up anytime. A little over an hour later, John walked into the ambulance service while I waited in the van. Within minutes, he returned and dropped a stack of papers in my lap.

"What's all this?" I said, confused.

"I don't know," John said, "He didn't say a word. He just handed me all these papers."

"It looks like he copied his whole file," I said, leafing through the pile.

The addendum was there along with Jack's death certificate, plus correspondence between Dr. Griffin and Roche Laboratories.

"Looks like our meeting might have shook him up a bit," I said.

"You think?" John said. "I hope it did shake him up, I mean *really* shake him up."

"I wonder why he just handed you these letters?" I said, scanning the documents but determined to wait until later to read them quietly. "There has to be a reason."

# TWELVE

*In the matters of truth and justice there is
no difference between large and small problems,
for issues concerning the treatment of people are all the same.*

ALBERT EINSTEIN

I ran through my front door, grabbed the phone, and dialed the television station to tell the producer the addendum was in hand. I'd read it several times in the van on the way home, but nothing clicked.

"What's it say?" he said.

"In a conference this morning including Coroner Tom Streams; Paul Lang, IUP police; and Anthony Antolik, Indiana Borough police, held in my office at 8:15 a.m., the toxicology report and autopsy findings and data indicate an alcohol-related death due to asphyxiation by aspiration of gastric contents. In addition, certain drugs of abuse were identified, however, the levels of these substances do not indicate a significant role in his demise," I said. "It's signed Steven P. Griffin, M.D. Pathologist, January 5, 1988."

"Bingo!" Samuels said. "Now you have it!"

"What do I have?" I said, feeling stupid.

"You have proof! There's no alcohol in his body at the time of his death, right?"

"Yes," I said, still staring at the document, befuddled.

"Now read it again," he said, excited.

Davis, Jack Allen                                          CA87-56

ADDENDUM REPORT

In a conference this morning including Coroner Tom Streams, Paul Lang -- IUP Police, and Anthony Atolik - Indiana Borough Police held in my office at 8:15 A.M. the toxicology report and autopsy finds on a Jack Allen Davis, Jr. were reviewed. The available findings and data indicate an alcohol related death due to asphyxiation by aspiration of gastric contents. In addition, certain drugs of abuse were identified, however, the levels of these substances do not indicate a significant role in demise.

SPG:jmh
0'/05/88

Steven P. Griffin, M.D.
Pathologist

Original autopsy addendum that states Jack's death was alcohol-related even after toxciology report returns with no alcohol detected in his blood at the time of death.

108

I read a few words, "Oh, I see! Even after the toxicology report comes back stating there's no alcohol detected in his blood, Dr. Griffin attributes his death to alcohol. That's what he told the coroner and other officials in his office that morning."

Coroner Streams repeated the doctor's words at the coroner's inquest a week later.

"Thanks," I said. "Please let me know as soon as you hear from Wecht."

"Any day now," he said, hanging up.

I didn't want to say anything in front of him but something else in the addendum confused me. The part about drugs brought back a comment Coroner Streams made during our interview.

"You know there were other drugs involved," he said after I questioned the blood alcohol level. "We didn't want to make that public for the family's sake."

I thought of Jack's parents. Not only did the county coroner tell them their son drank himself to death, now he was playing the drug card. Which, after reading the autopsy addendum sounded more like a veiled threat.

After dinner, I stretched out on the living room floor to figure out how the letters between Roche Laboratories and Dr. Griffin played into this case. Why did Streams just hand them to John?

On October 22, 1987, after performing the autopsy, Griffin sent a letter with body tissues from Jack's heart, liver and kidneys, plus urine and stomach content samples to Roche Laboratories.

"The patient is a college-aged male who was seen Friday evening having frequented several taverns and reportedly drank to excess. He was found dead late Wednesday afternoon without evidence of significant trauma but with emesis over the face, through the nostrils and on his clothing." Dr. Griffin requested alcohol and drugs of abuse testing.

"Since this is a case of rather acute forensic interest at this time, all due speed is requested in processing and reporting these results. Preliminary telephone collect calls will be honored."

On December 18, almost a month later, Dr. Griffin sends a second letter to the lab, asking why he hasn't received the final report promised weeks earlier.

"There is considerable concern from the coroner's office to resolve this case." Dr. Griffin wrote in his two-page letter. He recounted several calls made to the lab and still no report received.

"Continual pressure to complete this matter is mounting; so much so that the image of the hospital is being threatened according to our medical director, Dr. Kachik. Also, the image of Roche Biomedical Laboratories is being threatened, although you do not directly perform the testing."

Threatened how and by whom?

"Because of this mounting concern and continuing pressure to resolve this case, I must implore you to apply whatever pressure you can and bring this matter to a close."

Who was concerned and applying pressure? Certainly not the family who slunk home with their heads down and their tails neatly tucked between their legs. As far as I can tell they never looked back or demanded anything. Who wanted this case closed and fast?

National Medical Services, the lab that actually performed the tests, sent their response five days later on December 23. The letter outlined all tests conducted by toxicologist Lee N. Blum, Ph.D. with the results and an explanation for the delay in completing the report. There was also an additional note not included on the original toxicology report.

"The remainder of the specimens are scheduled to be discarded on February 8, 1988 unless arrangements are made prior there to."

The final letter Roche Laboratories sent to Dr. Griffin dated January 8, 1988, explains the extra testing performed. "The delay in reporting results was unusual. NMS evaluated your patient first for psychoactive substances and second for 'sudden death.' As a result, there was a delay of nine weeks in the report." The lab also promised the best possible service in the future.

The next day I called the lab to ask why they tested for "sudden death." Again, the supervisor recalled the case without hesitation. He said the lab could not figure out the results in this case. Trace amounts of alcohol turned up in the stomach and urine but not in the blood and one plausible explanation is he died instantly. Again, he referred me to Dr. Griffin for further explanation.

So based on scientific evidence, Jack had no alcohol in his blood at the time of death. However, based on Dr. Griffin's final addendum, which concluded his death was alcohol-related, the local bar was cited for serving alcohol to a minor. I really needed to get my hands on a copy of the citation to find out more about that case.

Made you wonder if all this happened to appease the family in some way or make a public case to uphold the coroner's alcohol-related death theory? Sounds sinister but that's where my mind headed after the comments about the body functioning after death.

The LCB cited the bar then filed the citation four days after the one-year deadline so the case was thrown out of court. Headlines in the newspaper made it look as if someone was being held accountable for Jack's death months later.

I placed another call to state Liquor Control Board (LCB) office in Punxsutawney with every intention of hounding the bureau chief to death to get a copy of the citation. No need, he scheduled an appointment with me for the next day and offered directions to his office.

Inspired, I immediately contacted the LCB attorney to find out how to go about getting a copy of the transcript of the appeal hearing. He rattled off the case number as well as the name and phone number of the court-reporting agency without hesitation.

One quick call, no muss, no fuss, the transcript was in the mail. If only everything were that simple! No word from Dr. Wecht yet, and I couldn't exactly hound the television producer. His promise to call as soon as he heard anything made my heart jump every time the phone rang.

I kept busy day and night. My mind raced constantly. Sometimes late at night as I sat quietly in my living room piecing together events of that day and planning the next, the incredible story unfolding before me hit me right between the eyes.

Thank goodness, a fellow reporter stopped by every once in a while to have a few beers at a neighborhood bar. He listened, shook his head and helped me figure things out on several occasions. He also kept me up on office gossip. I rarely went into the office except to file a story or work on other assignments.

For months I'd been living in my own world. A side of the world I'd never seen before up close and personal. Jack's death shoved harsh reality down my throat and ripped the rose-colored glasses off my eyes. I had to look at a truth I never wanted to see or believe about my fellow human beings. You can turn off the news, shut off the lights and go to bed. The dead bodies don't lie on the floor next to your bed demanding attention. I lost weight; bills piled up. I could not stop.

Did you ever open your eyes in the morning and think you're dreaming? The phone's ringing—ringing—ringing. It's real! Get up!

"I'm sorry," the television producer said. "I called Dr. Wecht; he's not ready to respond."

"Okay," I said, disappointed. "I guess you know how anxious I am to hear his opinion."

"Me, too," he said. "I hate to keep saying this to you but I'll call you as soon as I hear anything. I thought I'd give it a shot and call him. Maybe it will speed things up."

Acceptance and patience, the two biggest lessons you learn while conducting an investigation. I sighed, took a deep breath, stretched out on the couch, and closed my eyes for what seemed like minutes—RING!

"The university has decided to release the police report," the IUP Public Safety director said. "Do you want to give me an address so we can mail it to you?"

"No," I snapped. "We'll pick it up this afternoon."

"You're coming up here to get it?" he said, surprised. "Today?"

"You bet your Aunt Martha!" almost flew out of my mouth instead of an exuberant "Yes!"

I'd been waiting weeks to get my hands on the report and knew John would be roaring to go with me to pick it up. I don't know why, but for the first time, I felt scared. I told John about my fear, so he rustled up a friend and the three of us hit the road.

As soon as we walked up to the desk in the IUP Public Safety Office, the investigating officer handed me a form to sign. For some reason, my name was on the release, even though as you may recall, John signed and submitted the request letter. I turn to John with a quizzical look on my face.

"I think they've made a mistake," I said, handing the form to John. "Your name should be on this form. You're the one who made the request."

"You're right," John said. "Why is her name on the form?"

"It doesn't matter," the officer said. "It's just a formality. Someone has to sign for the report."

"Okay," I said, scribbling my name. "Here, John you sign, too. You made the request; it's your police report."

Luckily my instincts kicked in; later, IUP police threatened to arrest me for identifying myself as Jack's sister, which I never did. I identified myself as someone looking into his death for the family. Which, I assume, left everyone wondering who–and why someone was poking their nose into this stuff two years later. As you've seen, some were happy to see us, others not too pleased.

No matter. We jumped back in the van with the IUP police report in hand. Victory! I really didn't think they'd release it without a fight. Then again, why tempt negative publicity.

That night, I covered a school board meeting, filed my story, went home and climbed into bed around midnight. No need to breathe deeply to knock myself out this time; pure exhaustion took over. Abe Lincoln could have been lying on the floor next to my bed with a gigantic bullet hole in the middle of his forehead and I wouldn't have flinched. I fell sound asleep and experienced one of the incredibly vivid dreams I had during this investigation. I am sitting outside on a park bench with Jack. He is a young child, around age nine or ten. We're talking. He looks frightened, upset. I tell him we're doing our best and keep reassuring him that everything is going to be all right. He shakes his head back and forth, doubtful. I comfort him. Our conversation feels so real, I awake feeling strange but calm.

As soon as my feet hit the floor, my mind moves at breakneck speed. Things to do, documents to collect, details to decipher, data to compute, variables to consider, evidence to piece together, questions to answer—find the truth.

# THIRTEEN

*Justice is truth in action.*

Benjamin Disraeli

Things were looking up. I had the IUP police report in hand, and Dr. Wecht called the television station. He reviewed the toxicology and autopsy reports; confirmed Jack was *not* intoxicated at the time of death and called the autopsy performed in Indiana incomplete. Jack's skull had not been opened and examined. He could not determine any reason for Jack's death based on the reports.

"You were right!" the television producer said, very excited. "Would it be possible to set up a meeting for me with Jack's brother?"

"Sure!" I said, feeling light enough to fly. "He works nights. Would tomorrow afternoon work for you?"

We set a time and hung up. I jumped up and down all over my apartment whooping and hollering for at least fifteen minutes. What a relief! World-renowned forensic pathologist, Dr. Cyril Wecht validated my findings—at last! Having an expert on your side backing you up instead of sticking your neck out all alone makes a world of difference, especially during your first investigation.

I regained my composure somewhat then literally flew on cloud nine over to John's house to tell him the news in person. His face lit up as bright as a thousand candles! His nagging doubts over the past two years were justified; his little brother absolutely positively *did not* drink himself to death.

"How could they just lie to us like that?" he said, shaking his head in disbelief as he sped the van backwards out of his driveway. "Fry 'em! Fry the son of a bitches!"

We were on our way to meet with the state LCB bureau chief that afternoon, which turned into one of the happiest trips we'd made so far. John blasted Tom Petty singing, "I Won't Back Down" as the minivan wound up and around the snaky country roads. Every once in awhile we'd look at each other, smile, giggle and slap each other "high fives" along the way. Little did we know what lay ahead just over the horizon.

As soon as we reached the top of the hill leading down into the small town of Punxsutawney, we went over the rules again. I'd do the talking and John would listen and stay calm. The LCB bureau chief shook our hands as soon as we came through the door, ushered us into his office and closed the door. He pointed to two chairs situated side by side in back of the large wooden desk crammed into a very small room, and then took a seat opposite us.

"Mind if I ask what took you people so long to look into this?" he said, leaning forward and folding his hands in front of him on the desk while staring into our eyes. I can't speak for John, but I know the blood drained from my head and my jaw dropped almost to my chest. He handed John a copy of the citation filed against the bar.

"Here take this, too," he said, holding out another document. "This is a copy of the judge's final decision in this case. I could lose my job for giving you this. It's not public information."

We stared again, speechless.

"I've never seen anything like this in my twenty years on the force," the state trooper said, standing to shake our hands before showing us to the door. Dazed, we strolled back to the van, dumbfounded.

"He said he's never seen anything like this in his twenty years on the force," John mumbled as he turned the key in the ignition. "And did you hear him ask why it took so long for someone to look into this?"

No rants. John slowly backed the van out of the parking space then turned to look at me before pulling out of the lot. "This is unbelievable," he said, his face red, blue eyes as wide as saucers.

I had no idea how the documents he gave John fit into this case but the state trooper's words rang in my ears, "I could lose my job for giving you this."

I swear, this time I really did hear the eerie theme song from the 1950's television show, the *Twilight Zone* playing in the background as John drove back to Pittsburgh. I think we both felt as if we'd been having an out-of-body experience the entire day; everything felt so unreal. That morning, Dr. Wecht's opinion sent us soaring to the moon and back, and then the state trooper shocked the hell out of us after lunch. I hated to say anything to John after all that had happened but saw no alternative.

"I need to speak to Jack's parents now," I said softly as he turned into his driveway. John killed the engine and stared straight ahead for a few minutes before nodding his head. He had to know this moment would come sooner or later but still seemed worried. I was, too.

How would they feel about ripping open old wounds and reliving their pain? I dreaded this meeting from the start. At this point, however, I needed their input. They were there the moment Jack's body was found and could provide personal accounts concerning many events that followed.

John called a few hours later. They agreed to meet with me at Jack's father's house after dinner the next day. My insides trembled. Less than twenty-four hours to emotionally, intellectually, and physically prepare myself to present overwhelming information in as concise manner as possible to the parents of a murdered child. No pressure there. A lot to explain and many painful questions to ask parents who've been trying their best to come to terms with their son's death over the past two years.

I didn't expect them to be happy to meet me. John told them what we'd been up to for over a month now. I often wondered if they slept that night, I barely shut my eyes. Maybe, like John, Jack's parents hadn't sleep well for years. What did they think about the way their son supposedly died?

The good part was an expert had validated my findings and there were many more details to share with them now than if we'd met earlier. The timing seemed perfect. Plus, a state trooper and a magistrate had both urged us to investigate Jack's death and pieces of this bizarre puzzle were flying at me faster than I could fit them together.

That night as I sorted documents into neat piles, jotted down notes and put together a rough outline, I figured the most important thing to tell them was that their son had no alcohol in his body when he died.

Just the thought of meeting Jack's parents shook me to my core. What do you say to a mother and father living your worst nightmare, the death of a child? My mind raced with facts; my heart ached in sympathy. I needed to find a way to handle all the anxious feelings rushing through me. Keep busy, I thought, scanning the IUP police report for someone to call. How about one of the sorority girls who attended the party that night?

As the phone rang, I glanced at the clock and realized whoever answered might be pissed about my calling after nine at night. On the other hand, since all members of the sorority had refused to talk to police without an attorney present and were never questioned again, my hopes of getting anywhere with any of them seemed doubtful.

"Why weren't they ever questioned again?" I wondered, thinking their actions made them look guilty of something whether they were or not. The same held true for the only male student, who walked with Jack to the bar and was not a fraternity brother. He refused to talk to police without an attorney present and was never questioned again either.

The next day, I asked the IUP officer if not questioning those who refused to talk without a lawyer present is normal procedure.

"No," he said. "But it is up here."

After several rings, a young girl answered the phone. After listening to my pleas, she agreed to talk if not identified. She sounded shaky at first but once she got started let it all out.

"Jack came to the party with his fraternity brother. He really didn't know anybody there. I remember he was introduced to everyone as Jack, but the name on the front of his fraternity jacket was different and everyone teased him about having the wrong name and the wrong jacket."

Later she also saw Jack in the bar, doing "a lot of shots."

"He had a lot of money and was buying everyone drinks. He seemed happy," she said. "He was thrown out of the bar for fighting around eleven o'clock. He left with his big brother. That's the last time I saw him."

She paused, taking a few deep breaths before continuing.

"I was beaten up myself that night as I walked home with my boyfriend," the sorority girl said. "His name is John, he is a member of the Sig Tau, too. I had a black eye and my boyfriend was beaten up pretty good. There were a lot of fights going on that night between locals, fraternities and outsiders; people not from Indiana."

She described the scene that night as "crazy."

"There were drive-by shootings and both boys and girls were getting jumped and beaten up on the street. Some were beaten so badly they had to be life-flighted to Pittsburgh hospitals. After Jack's body was found, my boyfriend and I left school because we were so scared. We didn't know what was going on and no one told us anything."

I scribbled words down as fast as possible. Sure sounded like all hell broke loose in the streets the weekend Jack disappeared.

"That's all I want to say right now," she said and abruptly hung up. I tried contacting her again to ask more questions but she did not return my calls.

After a few fretful hours of sleep, the next morning I started calling helicopter companies and found the service provider for Indiana County on the first try. The woman who answered the phone looked up statistics for October 1987; twelve flights total, three the weekend Jack disappeared. For contrast, she also provided the number of life-flights for prior and following months, two in September and four in both November and

December. Which meant the number of life flights tripled that October.

What the hell happened? Drive by shootings, people beaten so badly on the streets they had to be life-flighted to Pittsburgh for treatment, plus all the fraternity fights reported in the paper that weekend. Did the major drug bust have anything to do with what happened in the small town that weekend? Retaliation? Was Jack a casualty? Why did he wear his big brother's fraternity jacket that night instead of his own? Then the really scary question popped into my head, "Was Jack a marked man?"

I remembered his roommate telling me, "Jack's big brother is known as one of the biggest cocaine dealers on campus."

Well, maybe his parents could shed some light on their son's activities back then. I decided not to mention anything about the fights during our first meeting. I had enough on my plate and knew the facts were hard to swallow.

"How will they react to me walking into their lives to pour salt in their wounds?" I wondered, watching out the window for John to pull up in the van that evening.

# FOURTEEN

*They are not dead who live in the
hearts they leave behind.*

Native American proverb

John pulled the minivan into a parking space and we both turned to look at Jack's father's small, white, row house for a few minutes before stepping out to cross the street. Jack Alan Davis, Sr. opened the door, greeted us, offered us chairs, walked to the couch and sat down next to Jack's mother, Elaine Davis-Lynch.

"I'll be out in a minute," Jack's stepmother, Lisa Davis yelled from the kitchen. John waited for her to come into the room before introducing me. She took a seat on the other side of her husband. We sat facing them, a knee-high wooden coffee table between us, polite smiles all around.

Lisa jumped up, nervously offering drinks, listed choices, then hurried back down the hall to the kitchen.

"John tells us you're a reporter," Jack, Sr. said. "We understand you and John have been looking into Jack's death."

"Yes," I said, providing some background information then explaining how John and I met. In the meantime, Lisa returned, placed a tray of drinks in front of us on the coffee table, and sat back down.

"I've talked to several experts and Dr. Cyril Wecht has confirmed my findings," I said. "I assume you've heard of Dr. Wecht?"

"Yes," they said, nodding in unison.

"Dr. Wecht confirmed yesterday that Jack was *not* intoxicated when he died," I said, waiting for a reaction. Instead, three stunned faces stared at me in silence. I held the toxicology report out across the table; Jack's father took it.

"I remember that," Elaine said. "I remember the coroner saying that at the inquest. He told us no alcohol was detected. A friend of ours was there. He's a doctor, and he questioned how they could say he was intoxicated when no alcohol was found in his blood."

Now I stared, dazed. Her lips moved but the words did not register in my brain, which kept shouting, "What? What'd she just say?" Thank goodness for tape recorders.

"I can't remember exactly what they told us. Something about the blood being rotten and it couldn't be tested. Something like that. We thought it was strange."

"You knew!" I said, finally able to form words again. "What exactly did they tell you?"

"I can't remember exactly what the coroner told us," Elaine said. "I know there was a long discussion about that and some other things at the meeting. Maybe I still have the tape. I taped the inquest. I'll see if I can find it for you."

I could have kissed her! She had the coroner's explanation on tape and promised to drop it off at Jack's father's house as soon as she could remember where she put it.

"Well," I said. "Dr. Wecht says Jack was not intoxicated and the autopsy is incomplete."

"I knew it! I just knew it!" Jack, Sr. said, his wide, blue eyes lit from inside. "I knew my son didn't die the way they said he did. He was not a big drinker. Whenever someone asked me about my son's death, I felt like I wanted to hide somewhere. Everyone at work knew what happened to Jack from the news."

He looked down at the floor, wringing his hands.

"I felt so guilty. I just wanted to disappear," he said, sniffing back tears. "I was ashamed to admit my son drank himself to death." He shook his head rapidly from side to side as if trying to wake from a horrible dream.

"I wanted a second autopsy," Lisa said, putting her hand on her husband's knee to comfort him. "I remember we talked about bringing his body back to Pittsburgh for a second autopsy. I kept saying we should bring him back."

She paused and looked sideways at her husband and Elaine for confirmation. They nodded.

"At one point," Lisa continued, "I think it was the coroner, told me to be quiet. They were so rude to me. Finally, we let it go. It was too painful at the time. We weren't exactly in our right minds, as you can imagine."

Elaine sat quietly listening with a far-away look in her eyes. Watching Jack's parents relive their pain hurt, but his mother affected me the most. I imagined her sorrow many times and the magnitude of her loss felt unbearable.

"How did she do it?" I wondered every time I looked at her. "How did she survive?

"Can you tell me exactly what happened when you went to Indiana," I said, looking from one face to another.

"I received a phone call from Officer Antolik of the Indiana Borough police department on Monday night," Elaine said, taking the lead. "One of Jack's roommates wanted to file a missing persons report and the officer wanted to know if he had my permission to do so."

She explained calmly and softly, "Since my son checked in with several people on a regular basis, I felt it was important to make a few inquiries before I gave my permission. I called his father and some friends who were like second parents to Jack. One of us always knew where he was. That's just the way Jack was. But none of us had heard from him since Thursday afternoon when he called to make a dinner date for the following Friday night."

She turned, looked towards Jack, Sr. and Lisa. They both nodded.

"I phoned Antolik back to say that we were also concerned and could I please speak with Scott, Jack's roommate. Scott explained the boys (roommates) went home for the weekend. The last they heard, Jack was going to a sorority party Friday night and there was a possibility he was going to drive up to Penn State to visit his cousin on Saturday and Sunday. But a phone call to his cousin proved Jack never made it there either. Scott said he was very concerned when Jack didn't go to any of his classes on Monday and the car his father gave him—which he protected with his life—was still parked where he left it Friday night to go to the party. This was all very uncharacteristic for Jack."

Early Tuesday morning, Elaine, Jack, Sr. and Lisa drove to Indiana to meet with Officer Antolik. They filed the missing persons report themselves, provided photographs of Jack and asked police what they could do to help find him.

"Antolik called IUP police to confirm Jack did not attend classes Monday," Elaine said. "Then drove us to Jack's car still parked in front of the sorority house. He took us inside and questioned some of the girls while we waited."

"Jack's fraternity brother, the one who went to the party with him, happened to walk past the car while we were there," Jack, Sr. said. "He told us about their adventures the night Jack disappeared."

"He happened by at that exact moment?" I thought, amazed, but said nothing.

"He also asked Jack (Sr.) to give him some things he'd left in the car that night," said Elaine. "Jack (Sr.) just opened the trunk and this kid took something out. We didn't even pay any attention. Now I wish I knew what he took."

Jack, Sr. and Lisa confirmed her memories with another nod of their heads.

"After that," Elaine continued, "Me, Jack (Sr.) and Lisa decided to drive around Indiana looking for some sign of Jack. We did that for about an hour and a half then went to the house where Jack lived and waited for word from the police. Antolik told us there were some young kids from out of town up there the night Jack disappeared, causing problems not only with students but causing property damage as well. One man was arrested, he said. The others headed back towards Pittsburgh. At this point, Antolik said there was a possibility that Jack had been abducted, perhaps not maliciously, but 'taken for a ride' anyway."

All three parents stared off into the distance as Elaine pieced together the sequence of events. Tuesday evening, they went back to borough police to file a missing persons report with the state. In the meantime, Jack's roommates went to the campus newspaper with his picture and asked that a story be published asking anyone to call who might have seen Jack since the previous Friday.

"The next morning my two step-sons drove up to help with the search," Elaine said. "They made posters with Jack's picture on them and passed them out all over town. Before noon, the last person that saw Jack alive called Officer Antolik to tell him how he walked Jack back to campus to find him a place to sleep in some dorm room because he was so drunk. Antolik said he still believed Jack was abducted."

Jack, Sr. and Lisa listened quietly as Elaine continued recalling their painful experience.

"We were pretty antsy by then," she said. "Some of our friends from Pittsburgh arrived to be with us during our wait. They were puzzled by the fact that no one had searched the campus and surrounding areas."

With the help of their friends and some recruited volunteer firefighters from Pittsburgh, Jack's parents formed their own search party.

"My stepson, Tom, called the state police to ask what was being done to find Jack. They said they didn't know anything about the missing IUP student," Elaine said. "That's when anger took over. Jack (Sr.) and Tom went to confront Antolik and find out why the state never received the missing persons report they filed. In the meantime, students began arriving at Jack's house. They came with flashlights, food and a huge pot of coffee. Jack (Sr.) and Tom told Antolik that we were about to search the campus and surrounding area and told him Indiana Borough police could either help or stay out of our way."

"You know," Jack, Sr. said. "I remember standing in that police office and they were trying to talk us out of doing a search because they thought it was a waste of time. Antolik asked us where we would even begin to look. I told them Jack could be anywhere. There were many stairwells and sort of like deep walkways under some windows around the buildings on campus. I told him, he could have fallen into one of them. It seems strange that that is exactly where he was found. It sticks in my mind now." Volunteers gathered on campus at the football field around ten Wednesday night, then dispersed into groups and headed off in different directions. Twenty minutes later, three of Jack's fraternity brothers found his body in the stairwell.

"Do you know how they told me about my son," Jack, Sr. said, shaking his head back and forth. "I was with a bunch of people searching on the other side of campus. A police car drove up and the officer said they'd found him. I was so excited as I walked up to the patrol car. 'He's dead' was all I remember the officer saying before I passed out. He was so cold! I still can't believe he was so cold! Can you believe it?"

Things looked different two years later. Disbelief showed on their faces along with the frantic wide-eyed startled look of people awakened from a sound sleep by someone banging on a metal cooking pot with a large wooden spoon. I didn't realize at the time that this was probably the first time they'd been together and discussed what happened during those traumatic days.

"I was back at Jack's house when police walked in and told me he was dead," Elaine said, sounding far off in another world. "My stepsons went with our friend, Dr. Ron Marshall to the stairwell. They wanted to see Jack for themselves."

"I saw the body after the police arrived," Dr. Marshall said during a phone interview a few days later. "I noticed there was no release of urine or fecal matter, which is what usually happens when someone dies. Everything lets go. You could see the displacement of skin tissue on the left side of his face from lying in that position. I remember thinking about seeing all that when they said he choked to death on his own vomit. I thought the vomit would have come out and cleared his air passages because of the way his head was turned to the side."

"I don't remember too much about that night. I was in shock," Elaine said. "I just remember sitting on the floor in Jack's house. I couldn't believe what was happening. It's like you're in some kind of nightmare. You hear voices and see people around you, but it all runs together until you finally shut down."

The next morning after the autopsy, IUP officials showed up at the house to tell them how Jack died.

"We could not believe what we were hearing," Jack, Sr. said. "I'd never heard of anyone dying that way before. It was so strange. They told us it happens all the time. What did we know?"

At some point, Jack's parents went to Indiana Hospital to make arrangements for his body to be transported to a funeral parlor back home in Penn Hills.

"His hand was sticking out from under this cover they had over him, " Lisa said. "I noticed a big bruise on his hand. When I saw the bruise, I thought something was wrong. That's when I kept saying we should get a second opinion. One of the officers told me to sit down and be quiet. That's what he said, 'Why don't you sit down and be quiet.' Can you believe it?"

Four years after our first meeting, Elaine sent me a "Thank You" note. She said, "I continue to beat myself up for being so stupid and gullible. I must admit that most of that time is a blur. I think I was just so much in shock. I don't remember making decisions, but I know I did. Please pardon me. I just had a good cry. But I do remember deep down the reason I didn't want a second autopsy—and it wasn't the money. I just didn't want anyone else dissecting my baby anymore."

I knew exactly how she felt. When my father, age 47, died from pancreatic cancer, we refused an autopsy for the same reason. It's not easy picturing a loved one cut into pieces.

I sympathized with Jack's parents many times during our meeting that night, but the reporter inside me maintained a professional distance. John, on the other hand, could be as dramatic as he wanted recounting his adventures in Indiana. He reenacted the magistrate making his "sour grapes" comment, hands waving in the air. However, his voice turned somber when he told them the state trooper asked why it took so long for someone to look into Jack's death.

"Let us know what's going on," Jack, Sr. said as we stepped onto the porch. Whew! My fingers ached from scribbling fast for hours. Thank goodness the batteries didn't run out on the tape recorder in the middle of our long meeting. I forgot to bring extras, which I now realize wouldn't have mattered one bit. To this day, I can still remember every word and the looks on their faces the first time we met.

The next day, Elaine called. She found the tape of the coroner's inquest and already made arrangements to have it transcribed. What a relief knowing Jack's parents were on my side ready and willing to help if needed. I picked up the package she left at Jack's father's house a few days later.

At the inquest, Coroner Streams called the toxicology report "a little confusing" and said he had to get pathologist Dr. Steven Griffin to explain it to him. He apologized for Dr. Griffin not being able to attend that day.

"They tested for all types of drugs known to man," Streams said. "There were three that came back positive: alcohol, cocaine, marijuana. We will take them one at a time."

Streams described the alcohol in Jack's stomach as a large amount, with a smaller amount in the urine, none in the blood.

"When I first saw this report I was confused as to why there was no alcohol indicated in the blood, when there was in the gastric contents and in the urine," Streams said. "When we met with Dr. Griffin for him to explain that to us, his interpretation of this was that the body metabolized during the time between death and when the body was found. The red blood cells and the white blood cells still continue to work, perhaps that would be a good way to say it, after death occurs."

He really did say the body continues to function after death–and in front of a room full of reporters! I was amazed. Not being a medical doctor himself, Coroner Streams had to rely on Dr. Griffin's explanations. Jack's parents, on the other hand, trusted the Indiana County Coroner, the public official.

"And over that period of time, which I remember was five days between the time of death and when the body was found, the body metabolized the bloodstream down to zero. There was no alcohol found in the bloodstream."

I read the words and still found the whole thing hard to believe. The body continues to function after death? I never came across that information in any biology, physics, physiology or anatomy classes taken to earn my degree. Not one professor ever mentioned the body functions in any way, shape or form after death. Think about it. If a body continues functioning after death, how and when would a person be declared dead?

Streams addressed the alcohol content in the stomach and urine again, restating "the body functioned after death" scenario as well as his contention that there was no way to determine the amount of alcohol in his blood at the time of death. "It was probably quite high but there is no way to quantify it," he said.

"I wonder where you're coming from," Jack, Sr. said after introducing himself. "Why would you say it was quite high when none was detected?"

"I based my assumption on the amount of alcohol found in the stomach contents and urine," Streams said.

I wanted to give Streams the benefit of the doubt as I read the transcript, however, the experts I contacted said the toxicology report showed scant amounts of alcohol in the stomach and urine; the amount equal to the alcohol content of less than one ounce of beer in the stomach, less than half that in the urine. You can sort of excuse Mr. Streams, the ambulance driver elected county coroner, based on medical ignorance and misinformation—but what about the doctor who completed years of medical school?

"I don't know how Jack got down into that stairwell," Streams said. "We're positive he was not placed there, he was not thrown there, he was not hit on the head and nobody carried him down there. He got down there, I'm sure, by his own means. How or why, I don't know. There was no indication of a struggle, dragging, certainly not a fall or that he had fallen over that cement wall. There were no marks, no cuts or bruises."

To this day, his statement amazes me. Look closely. First Coroner Streams admits he doesn't know how Jack got down into that stairwell, and then turns around in the next breath and says he's sure he got there by his own means. How could he be positive about anything?

He also told the family Jack did not die instantly.

"After inhaling stomach contents, death does not occur immediately. He would lie there in that kind of state for up to an hour, hour and a half before death became evident."

The lengthy inquest involved the discussion of drugs, which Streams said he did not believe contributed to Jack's death. He also answered general questions about the stairwell, the search for Jack's body and other details about the case.

The transcript ended in the middle of a sentence. The tape ran out. Apparently, Elaine didn't notice.

# FIFTEEN

*If we could sell our experience for what they cost,
we'd be millionaires.*

ABIGAIL VAN BUREN

Now that I had met Jack's parents, I could easily imagine the looks on their faces when Coroner Streams announced that no alcohol was detected in their son's blood at the time of death, then told them, "It was probably quite high but there is no way to quantify it."

They were probably as confused as I was at that moment. Of course, I knew the body stops functioning after death, that's basic biology, but as a reporter I also know that facts have to be checked and rechecked. Even though I had never met or talked to Dr. Wecht before, I desperately wanted to hear what he'd say about Coroner Streams's comments at the inquest.

After pacing around the living room several times to summon courage, I dialed his number. Would the world-renowned forensic pathologist stop to talk to me? He didn't know me from a cake of soap. I explained the situation to his secretary; she put me on hold for about a minute, then Wecht picked up. I referred to the case, my connection to the television station, and then dove into specifics.

"You saw the toxicology report which states no alcohol was detected in his blood at the time of death. Well, the doctor who performed the autopsy told Coroner Streams the reason no alcohol was found is because the alcohol metabolized out of the body after death. Is that true? Can the body metabolize the alcohol out of the blood after death?"

"What?" he screamed so loud my hand automatically jerked the phone away from my ear. "Who said that?"

"The doctor who performed the first autopsy in Indiana," I said, surprised by his frankness and trying not to giggle.

"The fucking asshole! Tell me exactly what he said."

I read the exact words from the transcript about the red and white blood cells metabolizing the alcohol out of his blood after death.

"I never heard anything like this in my entire life!" Dr. Wecht yelled. "Fucking asshole! He actually said that to the family? That's impossible! This is a medical doctor who said this? What's his name?"

"Dr. Steven Griffin," I said.

"I'd like to know where he went to medical school!" Dr. Wecht said. I thanked him, hung up, and immediately called Elaine to tell her what happened.

"Maybe you should set up an appointment to talk with Dr. Wecht in person," I said. She agreed, but only if I'd go with her since I knew more about the case than she did. After a moment's hesitation, I said I'd go but explained I could not be involved in any capacity other than as a reporter, the word "objectivity" steadfast in my mind.

Deep in my heart, however, I teetered on a very fine line. Of course, there are always two sides to every story; it just so happened in this case one outweighed the other, throwing things off balance. Why in the world did this medical doctor tell not only the traumatized family their son's body continued to function after death but police, the public and university officials? Did they all believe him?

The television producer called that afternoon to discuss running the story. He said the story would take three weeks to produce, they'd pay me $250, and I'd have no further input.

"That's the way it is and that is all we can pay for a story," he said. "Otherwise, it would be called checkbook journalism."

"You have to be kidding!" I thought to myself. "This is my baby!" Of course, I wanted maximum exposure but handing over months of hard work for someone else to complete—no way! Plus, offering me $250 for working at least a zillion hours felt like a slap in the face. I needed money; the rent was due.

"I can't do that," I said. "I really am grateful for all your help but I have to say no." Saying yes felt wrong. There had to be another way to get this story the public attention it deserved. A few minutes later, Elaine called to say she had an appointment with Dr. Wecht at two the next day and gave me directions to his office. I have to admit to being excited at the prospect of meeting him in person and hearing firsthand his professional opinion about this case.

We were seated around a very large, wooden table in Wecht's conference room. Jack Sr., Lisa, and John on my left, Elaine and her mother on the right. Wecht sat at the head of the long table; I faced him at the opposite end. He reviewed the toxicology and autopsy reports again, reconfirmed Jack was not intoxicated at the time of death and called the autopsy incomplete. Jack's head and neck were never opened and examined.

He said there was no way to determine how Jack died, then suggested exhuming his body for a second autopsy. In order to do so, he told the family, new facts had to be presented to the Indiana County district attorney, along with a formal request to exhume his body.

"He'll have to agree, which means the county would have to foot the bill," Wecht said. "So, it is hard to say how willing they'll be to do this. However, it looks like the only way now to determine how Jack died. Then, you might have a better understanding in order to find out why."

We all sat quietly, eyes glued on the man with all the power.

The family retained Dr. Wecht as their medical examiner and attorney. The fact that he was an attorney, too, surprised me. Now they had a medical examiner and attorney all rolled into one to help them find the truth. Jack's grandmother paid the retainer fee and Wecht gathered medical reports, microscopic slides, photographs, and other pertinent information, which set the ball spinning in a new direction.

No one could bring their son back, but maybe they'd be able to find some peace of mind and justice. Just knowing they had an expert of Wecht's caliber on their side put faint smiles on their faces as they filed out of his office that day.

That night, a reporter from the *Tribune-Review*'s Greensburg office called me out of nowhere. Apparently, my fellow reporter in the Pittsburgh office, in whom I had confided over a few beers, discussed the story with her behind my back. She heard I turned down the television offer and wanted to meet. I didn't know how to respond since the editor seemed disinterested in the story. She told me not to worry; she'd handle everything.

I felt awkward walking into the main office to meet with her the next day. We sat alone at a small table in the lunchroom, discussing details. At one point, the editor strolled in, poured himself a cup of coffee, glanced sideways at us a couple of times, then walked away without saying a word. We talked for quite awhile before I agreed to work with her. As we shook on it, she told me to leave the rest up to her.

The next morning, she said the editors wanted a second opinion from a different forensic pathologist. "There was some bad blood between the paper and Wecht. So, they want the opinion of their own expert before running any story about this case. We'll make all the arrangements."

With nothing to lose and everything to gain, I agreed. I'd be paid a fair price for my work as a freelance reporter once the paper published the story.

That afternoon, a large, thick brown envelope arrived in the mail. The transcript from the Pennsylvania Liquor Control Board appeal hearing turned out to be much bigger than I expected, at least fifty pages or more. I poured a glass of iced tea, settled in on the couch, and read the lengthy document word for word. Around page ten, I understood why the state LCB bureau chief said he'd never seen anything like this during his twenty years on the force.

The one and only witness to testify against the bartender at the original hearing held in front of Magistrate Orendorff took the stand almost a year later at the citation appeal hearing against the bar. Out of twenty students who told police they saw the bartender serve Jack alcohol, he was the only one willing to bear witness.

The student tells the court he saw the bartender pour and serve alcoholic beverages to the minor, Jack Alan Davis, Jr. in the bar the Friday night in question. On cross, the defense attorney questions his credibility based on his inability to identify the bartender at the first hearing in front of Magistrate Orendorff.

In response, the state LCB attorney calls the hearing "tainted and unethical" and encourages the witness to tell the judge what happened at the bartender's hearing.

"I was tricked into identifying the wrong bartender," the student said, explaining the extenuating circumstance to state LCB Administrative Law Judge Felix J. Thau.

Apparently, a man dressed in a suit and tie walked into the courtroom accompanied by the defense attorney and they sat next to each other at the defense table. When the student took the stand, the defense attorney showed him eight pictures of men with similar facial features, such as dark hair, mustaches, etc. Headshots of the fake bartender seated at the defense table as well as the real bartender—standing out in the hall—included. The actual defendant, the accused bartender, was not even in the courtroom!

"So, what I believe he (the defense attorney) did was lead me to believe the impostor was the real bartender. He was playing with my mind. I was very confused," the student said. "I knew he wasn't the bartender. I realized as soon as I said it that he was not the person. I realized what happened, okay? He ran a game on me and I fell for it. I was wrong. I knew I chose the wrong person."

Now let me get this straight. The Pennsylvania Liquor Control Board charges the bartender for serving alcohol to a minor, which according to Dr. Griffin contributed to his death. The state prosecutor whose entire case rests on his one and only eyewitness pointing out the accused—and the prosecutor knows exactly who he is prosecuting—doesn't question why the defendant is not in the courtroom? Isn't a bench warrant usually issued for the defendant's arrest for failure to show up at the scheduled hearing? The prosecutor had to know the defendant wasn't in the courtroom!

Hold on to your hats because this gets even more bizarre. The Indiana County district attorney refused to prosecute the case, claiming the state Liquor Control Board did not provide adequate notification of the scheduled hearing. So the state trooper who investigated the case stepped in as prosecutor.

To top it all off, when asked about the fake bartender, the magistrate said he didn't know the defendant was not in the courtroom that day.

"If I knew he wasn't there, I would never have held the hearing," Orendorff said. "You know, however, that if the bartender was out in the hall and not in the courtroom the prosecutor had to agree to that arrangement. It was with the permission of the prosecutor."

Which means, a state trooper with no legal background walked into the court room to prosecute a state Liquor Control Board case based on the testimony of one eyewitness—then to make it really tough for his star witness—agreed with the defense attorney to let the accused bartender stand out in the hall?

As I leafed through several pages of the court transcript, the LCB bureau chief's words rang in my ears. "I have never seen anything like this during my twenty years on the force." The LCB investigator contacted all twenty witnesses named in the police report who claimed to have seen Jack served alcohol in the bar. Their names are listed on page after page in the transcript, along with the investigator's comments.

The majority of the witnesses were "unavailable for questioning." Others asked to come to the office for interviews never showed. Out of the few the investigator managed to contact, all but the one who took the stand said they were mistaken and recanted their statements.

At one point, the judge asked the investigator if there was any reason that he could determine why the citation against the bar was filed four days after the one-year deadline. The state trooper replied there was no particular reason. The case against the bar was dismissed.

"We take the one-year provision of the Liquor Code Section 471 as a statute of limitations. A statute of limitations is considered an affirmative defense. As such, where a licensee does not raise the issue, we are loath to dismiss," LCB Judge Felix J. Thau said in his final decision. "The record is devoid of any information as to why the bureau issued the citation a full nine months after the investigation was completed."

The state trooper told Judge Thau his investigation ended February 8, 1988, a date that stuck out in my mind as I read the words. You know how you see something familiar but can't place it no matter how hard you try—then bingo! That was the exact same date that Roche Laboratories noted on the toxicology report for the scheduled disposal of specimens from Jack's body.

I couldn't help but wonder why the LCB ended the investigation in February, nine months before the one-year deadline, considering they only had one witness out of so many "unavailable" possibilities, not counting no-shows.

Since we met, I had contacted Elaine to help fill in blanks on several occasions. This time, I asked if she ever heard anything about the hearings held against the bar or bartender.

"They sent me a letter asking me to attend," Elaine said over the phone. "It was like they wanted me to be there to see what was going on or that they were going to do something that looked like justice. It was a real circus."

She recalled standing outside the magistrate's office with a friend who wanted to smoke a few cigarettes before the hearing started.

"It was really strange. This white limousine kept pulling up at the same corner about a block or so away from the magistrate's office. I remember we commented to each other about how much each guy that got out of the limousine looked so much alike. They were all dressed in suits and ties. They all had dark hair and mustaches and similar builds. We thought it was really strange. I hate to say it but it looked like they were all members of the Mafia," she said, lowering her voice to a whisper.

"There was only one kid that would testify. They gave him the business. I never saw anything like it. They showed him these pictures and apparently, he picked out the wrong person. I think they invited me there to see the show."

Elaine didn't know anything about the bar being cited or the hearing. Not wanting to go into detail, I told her the LCB cited the bar for serving alcohol to a minor and the case was dismissed on a technicality.

"I guess it fell through a loophole, I mean crack," I said, echoing the state LCB bureau chief's own words.

# SIXTEEN

*Justice consists not in being neutral between right and wrong,
but in finding out the right and upholding it,
whenever found, against the wrong.*

THEODORE ROOSEVELT

Needless to say, there were many cracks in this case and keeping track of all the twists and turns became a full time job. So far, I knew Jack had attended a sorority party with his fraternal big brother Friday night, wearing his big brother's fraternity jacket instead of his own. He left the party and walked to a bar, got kicked out for fighting, crossed the street to another bar, met this kid who supposedly walked him back to campus because he was drunk; five days later his body was found in a campus stairwell.

Following an autopsy the next morning, the county coroner ruled his death accidental and without scientific evidence concluded Jack walked into the stairwell, passed out from drinking too much alcohol, and choked to death on his own vomit. Two months later, the toxicology report states that no alcohol was detected in Jack's blood at the time of death. Still, the coroner announces at the inquest that the amount of alcohol was high at the time of his death but could not be determined for two conflicting reasons: one, the blood was rotten and could not be tested, and/or two, the blood *was* tested but alcohol was not detected because the body continued functioning after death, metabolizing the amount down to zero.

The state Liquor Control Board conducted an investigation until the exact day the specimens from the victim's body were destroyed at the lab. The bar is cited and its bartender is charged for serving alcohol to a minor. In court, the only eyewitness was tricked into identifying a fake bartender while the real bartender stood out in the hall with the permission of the state trooper who prosecuted the case. The citation against the bar is dismissed because it is filed nine months after the investigation ends but four days past the one-year deadline.

Who could make this stuff up? When I explained the details to others, which happened often, they looked doubtful to say the least. Sometimes I had a hard time believing myself. So, the minute I saw the look on my fellow reporter's face when we got into her car that morning to drive to West Virginia, I knew she had her doubts.

The paper set up an appointment for us to meet with a forensic pathologist at the University of West Virginia in Morgantown. We whited out all identifying information in the toxicology and autopsy reports in order to elicit a purely impartial evaluation of the documents, just in case the pathologist heard or read about Jack's death in the news.

"What do you think he is going to say?" the reporter said during the two-hour drive.

"Exactly what Wecht said," I replied, stomach muscles tightening. Who knows what anyone will say? I knew the truth, but sometimes doubted myself.

The white-haired man dressed in a white lab coat and green scrubs sat directly across from us at a table in a very large room that looked like a cafeteria. His half-frame reading glasses perched on the bridge of his nose as he read the reports.

"From these reports, there is no way to determine why this person is dead," said Dr. James Frost, deputy chief medical examiner for the state of West Virginia. "This person could not have been intoxicated at the time of death and the autopsy is incomplete because the skull and neck were never examined."

After he made his initial analysis, I explained the Indiana County Coroner's theory. Dr. Frost moved his head from side to side, disagreeing with every word I spoke.

"How can you find a body at the bottom of a concrete stairwell and not open the skull to see if there are any injuries? Like I said, there is no way to determine how this person died. He was unconscious due to alcohol? Where's the proof?"

"You knew what he was going to say, didn't you?" my fellow reporter said, glancing at me with a sly grin on her face as we sped down the highway. I just smiled, another validation under my belt. My stomach felt much calmer on the way home.

Two days later, we interviewed another forensic pathologist for the paper. My fellow reporter again glanced at me with the same knowing grin on her face as the second expert said the exact same thing as the other two. She believed me now.

The next day, the editors approved the story.

"What do you want me to do next?" she said, eager to get started.

A wave of calm, starting at the top of my head, traveled slowly down my body, melting the tense muscles in my face, my neck, across both shoulders, and my chest. The feeling traveled into my stomach, down each leg, all the way to my toes. I had help, someone to work with, who believed and understood.

"I still need the Indiana Borough police report," I said. "They told John to get a subpoena."

"Don't worry about it," she said, making me feel as light as a feather. "I'll take care of that right now. It's public information and that falls under the Freedom of Information Act. They can't refuse to give me that report."

"I'd also like you to set up an interview with Dr. Steven Griffin," I said. "I'll write questions for you to ask when you're ready."

"Alright," she said. "I'll call you later."

I felt grateful, happy and exhausted. I had a council meeting to cover that night and Jack's family wanted me to accompany them to an appointment with Dr. Wecht the next day. We met at his office around two, went back into the same conference room, and everyone took the same seats.

"I cannot emphasize this enough," Wecht said. "The biggest problem we have is that Jack's skull and neck were never opened. A person can have internal head injuries without any outward indications. I would suggest his body be exhumed and a second autopsy be performed—but that is up to you people."

He looked around the table, making eye contact with each family member.

"You're the only ones who can make that request of the Indiana County district attorney. He will have to approve it. I would like to think that they'll be cooperative but I doubt that will be the case. Like I said, Indiana County would have to foot the bill and I don't know how willing they'll be to pay for this."

He reassured them that Jack was not intoxicated at the time of death then dropped a new bomb. After examining the microscopic slides of Jack's lung tissue he received from Dr. Griffin, he could also conclude that Jack did not die from asphyxiation.

"In order to conclude that a person died from asphyxiation you must find the gastric contents in the air sacs of the lungs. It's just not here," Wecht said. "So the question now is how and why did Jack end up in the stairwell dead?"

Dr. Wecht told the family he went to Indiana to examine the stairwell and ask questions. He could not believe that no one saw his body lying there for five days. Also, after examining slides of Jack's body tissue and seeing photographs, he said the body was not in a state of decomposition one would normally expect to find in a body that had been dead for five days. That's when Wecht pulled the pictures out of a large, brown envelope.

"Upon careful examination of these photographs taken of the body in the stairwell, I can say that Jack had at least a three-day beard growth on his face. We need to know if anyone saw him and can verify he was clean shaven the night he disappeared."

I scribbled notes as fast as possible, and glanced over every once in a while to make sure the tape in the recorder kept spinning.

"It is possible that he lay unconscious in the stairwell for some reason and during those five days the alcohol did metabolize out of his body very slowly," Wecht said. "However, the large amount of stomach contents described in the autopsy and noted in the toxicology report indicates this is not a possibility. If the alcohol slowly metabolized out of the body then the stomach contents would also have been slowly digested out of the stomach over the five-day period."

We stared, speechless.

"The amount of stomach contents points to two things. First, he ate some sort of meal at least five hours before his death because that is how long it takes the stomach to empty after a meal, and he did not vomit because the amount found would have been considerably less."

He stopped and looked at each parent, I guess to see if they were still coherent. This was a lot to digest in minutes. Not intoxicated, did not vomit and choke to death, not dead for five days. Which meant he was alive somewhere, apparently well enough to eat and eliminate body waste—no urine and feces were found on his body or clothes—but could not shave?

I knew from nursing, unconscious patients lying in bed continue to move their bowels and urinate. If he laid unconscious anywhere for five days metabolizing anything out of his body there would have been urine and feces all over the place. That's a fact!

My mind raced in so many directions as my fingers tried to capture every word the doctor spoke. If he didn't choke on his own vomit, how did he die? And, more importantly, how did he end up in a stairwell about a block away from the spot the last person supposedly left him five days before?

"Have you people seen these photographs?" Wecht said, looking around the table. I froze like a deer caught in the headlights.

"I don't know if you would want to see them, but they are here if you want to take a look," Wecht said. "Let me just warn you, they're not pleasant."

They looked at each other, then back at me.

"Oh God!" I screamed inside my head. "Don't look! You don't want to see those horrible pictures!" Tears fill my eyes as I write these words years later.

"I want to see them," Elaine said.

I wanted to run out of the room, crawl under the table; my body switched into fight-or-flight mode with no escape!

"Do you want to see them, too?" Dr. Wecht said, reaching towards Jack's father with photos in hand. He took the stack of black-and-white photos, glanced at each one for a few seconds, then handed it to his wife next to him. Lisa took her turn and reached across the table, passing them to Elaine, who studied each one carefully, then handed them to Jack's grandmother.

Around the table the photos went, John and I watching the procession. We'd seen them once and that was more than enough for both of us. Instead, I watched their faces as they stared at the gruesome photos with no signs of emotion or change in expressions. I could not imagine being in their shoes for one second.

Elaine sat so close to me on my right, I could see the pictures over her shoulder as she studied each one. I had to look away, staring at the hundreds of books stacked neatly on shelves around the room, at Wecht, at the ceiling. When I looked back at Elaine, she still held pictures in her hand. She stared at the one of her son's naked body lying on a cold, gray, steel examination table with a great big, bloody hole where his chest used to be. Tears stung my eyes, knowing she'd never forget those images for as long as she lived—and neither would I.

"His clothes were not wet when they found his body," Elaine said, breaking the long silence. "It rained all day the day before they found his body. We walked around in the rain all day and we were soaked. When they gave us his clothes they weren't even damp. They don't look wet in these pictures, either."

"Can you get me the weather report for those five days in October?" Wecht said, looking at me. "Call the weather bureau. They'll have that information."

The pictures continued circulating around the table. As Elaine examined the picture of Jack in the stairwell after the police turned his body over on its side, I noticed his left leg sticking up frozen in mid-air. Come to think of it, I noticed the same strangeness in another picture. He's on the examination table dressed in his street clothes before the autopsy, and his right arm is frozen at a right angle across his body about two inches above his chest. His left leg is also still bent up in the air.

"How long does it take for rigor mortis to set in?" I asked Dr. Wecht. "His body is stiff in some of these pictures."

"Rigor mortis sets in about twelve hours after death," he said. "It's a slow process that involves a chemical reaction in the muscles of the body. This reaction causes the muscles to slowly contract and the body becomes very rigid. Then, it takes another twelve hours for the body to relax or go limp."

"Would that mean he wasn't dead twenty-four hours when his body was found?" I said. "Or maybe even less, twelve hours?"

He looked down at the pictures, up at me. "I think you have your answer."

"Oh no!" I thought, the family staring at me. That means Jack was alive and breathing somewhere as they desperately searched all over town looking for him.

"Unfortunately, there is a two-year statute of limitations on filing wrongful death and negligence law suits," Dr. Wecht said. "You could have filed wrongful death against the university and claimed negligence against the bar, the doctor, whoever. So, it isn't going to do you any good now. It would have been a good way to get some answers in this case."

They were five months too late.

"I think we just pissed away two thousand dollars," Jack's father muttered under his breath on the way out the door.

John's face turned bright red; he could go off any second. Thankfully, he waited until we reached the parking lot to blow his top.

"That asshole! Where was he for sixteen years? He comes back and starts acting like a father when Jack turns sixteen. He gives him a car and acts like all of a sudden he is the loving daddy. Bullshit! He's only here for the money. He thought we were going to be able to sue for millions of dollars. He wanted his share. That's all he is here for—not Jack. I can't even stand to look at him. I'd like to punch him right in the face."

Use to his outbursts, I drove away without saying a word. I had to hand it to John. He didn't hold anything back and probably didn't have stomach problems like I did. My reaction was to crawl into bed for a much-needed nap, then toss and turn every which way, too stressed to fall asleep.

No alcohol and he didn't choke to death on his own vomit. Where was he for five days? Was Indiana Police Chief Antolik right from the start? Was Jack abducted?

# SEVENTEEN

> *At his best, man is the noblest of all animals;*
> *separated from law and justice he is the worst.*
>
> Aristotle

Knowing Jack did not choke to death on his own vomit and lie in that stairwell for five days sent us back to Indiana, searching for new leads just about every day. In the evening, I dialed phone numbers listed in the IUP police report, hoping to reach anyone willing to shed light on Jack's last few days on earth.

After several wrong numbers, a few hang-ups, and some dead ends, one former student said flat-out she did not want to be involved for fear of retaliation by Jack's fraternity.

"But you don't go to school there anymore," I said, hoping to allay her fears.

"I'm still afraid," she said then ended the conversation.

Her comments lead me to take the advice Jack's roommate had offered months before about focusing on the fraternity.

Elaine said she knew very little about them and suggested I talk to Jack's former high school teacher and his wife, "Jack's second parents." She said he spent his last summer helping them with their side business selling T-shirts in Virginia Beach.

"He worked with us during the summer. He was a super kid," his former high school teacher said that night on the phone. "He started coming to our house to visit when he was in seventh grade. He'd come in and make himself completely at home. We bought him clothes and I can't tell you how many times Jack spent Christmas with us. We were very close. I can't tell you enough good things about him."

Pause, he cleared his throat.

"He was majoring in business, restaurant management to be exact. We were very proud of him. We were very upset when Jack told us he joined a fraternity."

Jack enrolled at the university a few weeks early to catch up on a few subjects before starting his freshman year. He met members of the fraternity while living in the dorm.

"By the time he told us, he was already going through initiation," he said. "We were very, very upset. I told him it would be expensive and require a lot of his time. Time he should dedicate to studying."

He suggested I talk with his wife and handed her the phone.

"My husband talked to him many times about not joining a fraternity in his freshman year," she said. "We heard they are a very violent fraternity. Someone told us that during one initiation ritual they got Jack drunk and cut his chest with a knife. I never saw any scar but that's what we were told and I always wondered if it was true."

She said she felt uncomfortable talking about this with anyone.

"There are many things that bother me when I look back at the week before his death. I never really put the pieces together until after his death," she said. "We got these weird phone calls from him several times before he died. I remember discussing the calls with my husband and saying, 'He wants us to tell him to come home.'"

"What exactly did Jack say?" I asked.

"He'd call out of the blue and ask if he had to come home that weekend to work. We didn't know why he was asking us but we knew instinctively we were supposed to say he had to come home. We got the feeling someone was there listening to the conversation when he made these calls. This happened a few times. We just played along."

Jack also called the Tuesday before he disappeared.

"He never called us with his problems," she said. "He called that day and said he didn't have any money to buy food and asked if we could help him. He said he was having bad headaches. He didn't call often to ask for food or money."

The couple brought Tylenol, took him to a restaurant for dinner, picked up a few bags of groceries and gave him thirty dollars the next day.

"When I look back at that night, I realize now something was wrong," she said. "We pulled up in front of his house a little after nine that night. He started to get out of the car, stopped, and began talking about his high school days and asking about old friends. He asked about different people and whether we'd heard anything about them. He got out of the car and got back in. He did this more than three times."

Pause, deep breath and sigh; her voice grew sadder with each word.

"Jack kept talking and telling us about how much time he spent in the library studying. It seemed like he was just looking for something to talk about and didn't want to get out of the car. Finally, I told Jack to please go inside before my husband falls asleep at the wheel. Jack got out again, turned and said, 'I love you Mrs. K.' I said, 'I love you, too, Jack.' That was the last time we saw him. It was the last time."

When Elaine told her she found the grocery bags untouched on his bedroom floor after his death, the memory of Jack's odd behavior, his comments, the strange phone calls, everything came flooding back.

"I remember him telling me he was so happy he found a house to live in that term. He said he was happy to get away from the fraternity and live with kids that weren't involved," she said. "I remember at the funeral his fraternity came in all wearing black arm bands, I remember thinking they looked like some kind of gang."

The wife of Jack's former high school teacher also recalled hearing a rumor that Jack used cocaine.

"He was very athletic and very particular about his body. He was a track star, you know. He worked out all the time to keep in shape. Jack would never put that stuff in his body."

"I heard that, too," I said. "Is there anything else you'd like to tell me?"

"I have so many memories of this boy," she said. "There isn't a day goes by I don't look at his picture and wonder what happened to him. It was a senseless death and I'm trying to learn to put it on the shelf. Every time I walk by his picture I ask, 'What happened to you?' There's no answer. I hope someone can find the answer."

"I hope so, too," I said, promising to give Elaine her best wishes the next time we spoke.

I leafed through my notes and found a few names we had copied out of old IUP yearbooks in the library. Jack's fraternity pledge book also had names with phone numbers. Members wrote messages on separate pages in the small, blue, spiral-bound notebook to encourage Jack, the "unknown goon" to stay strong during initiation.

Most scribbled notes promised fun as soon as he finished pledging; however, one message, in light of current circumstances, gave me the chills.

"Remember you only get out what you get in. Don't be DEAD WEIGHT!" The words "DEAD WEIGHT" underlined several times.

Pretty ominous words now, I had to call the number under the name to ask about the message.

"That didn't mean anything," Jack's fraternity brother said. "I was just encouraging him to get involved. That's all it meant."

"You realize how this looks after what happened," I said. "I just wanted to hear what you had to say."

"We were so upset about what happened to Jack. We got together and bought a memorial plaque, you know with his name on it. It's under a tree in front of the stairwell. If you go there, you'll see it."

As soon as our conversation ended, I made an appointment to speak with the university's director of student affairs the next day. For the first time, I made the trip to Indiana alone. No sense dragging John along to ask general questions; he needed sleep.

"Can you tell me anything about Sigma Tau Gamma fraternity?" I said, pushing the button on the tape recorder and setting it on an end table next to his chair.

"They have a criminal record as long as my arm," Terry Appolonia, IUP Director of Student Affairs said. "Unless someone comes in and specifically asks about this organization, our hands are tied. We can't stop anyone from joining any organization they choose. It's their constitutional right."

He explained the fraternity lost its national charter due to disorderly conduct the year before Jack pledged. The Recognized Organization Review Board, made up of students, took action after Sigma Tau Gamma members broke into another fraternity house and "inflicted extensive damage." They also ordered the fraternity to pay restitution.

The university formally denounced the group in a letter dated November 25, 1986. "Effective immediately, Sigma Tau Gamma is no longer recognized as an IUP organization...I'm obligated to inform you that, should any members of the fraternity, individually or in concert with others, attempt to threaten retaliation against any parties to these judicial proceedings, full criminal prosecution will be sought."

All this meant is the now "unrecognized fraternity" was not required to submit a membership list or comply with the minimum rules governing fraternities as outlined in the university code.

As Appolonia spoke, posters John and I had seen inside the library and stuck on poles around campus came to mind. The group still advertised and recruited students on campus.

"Isn't that Jack's fraternity?" I had said, as we stood studying the cartoon-like drawing of a large building with "IUP" printed across the top and "SUTTON" over the doors.

"That's the administration building," I said. "Look at that guy standing on the roof, he looks like a giant compared to the building." A very muscular male cartoon character wearing a muscle T-shirt with the words "TAU TOUGH" on the front, stood with exaggerated muscles bulging in his legs and arms. His arms flexed above his head and slightly parted legs made the character look firmly planted in a body-builder's competitive pose. "TAUS" in bold, two-inch print headlined the poster, with the words "Enough said..." in smaller print to the left of the building, with open rush dates, time and location written on the left.

Another poster showed a Yosemite Sam cartoon-type character standing on top of the word "TAUS" printed in large letters. He was shooting two guns downward to shatter the letters. The words, "HONOR...INTEGRITY...PRIDE...AND A LITTLE BIT OF FUN" coming out of his mouth. "MORE THAN A FRATERNITY...A WAY OF LIFE!" was printed across the bottom. Rush dates, times and events were also included.

"Withdrawal of recognition does not guarantee the disbanding of the group," the IUP Director of Student Affairs explained. "That informal social group can continue to function as a group of men. They can choose to call themselves a fraternity, and for the most part, due to the ignorance of the public, if you rush, pledge, mix with sororities, and use Greek letters to define yourself, you are perceived as a fraternity."

Sounded like a catch twenty-two. The university had a group of guys calling themselves a fraternity, wearing same color jackets, and recruiting pledges on campus. No rules, no charter, no one to monitor their membership or behavior. And here was the catch, even though the university does not recognize the group as a fraternity, their presence on campus implied association and legitimacy.

"The university makes no attempt to inform students about unrecognized fraternities but does provide students who ask with a list of recognized organizations," Appolonia said. "It's a civil rights issue. Like I said, we can't stop anyone from joining any group."

So freshman students, such as Jack, looking to make friends, connect, belong and be accepted in their new environment, pledge alliance to the renegade fraternity, not knowing the difference.

"We've had incidents of alleged sexual assaults where women claim to be at their parties and assaulted," the director said. "We hear complaints and allegations regularly from students who are in a bar or local establishment and have been physically or verbally assaulted by this group. Their behavior still reflects on the university, the Greek systems, and the student body."

He slowly shook his head back and forth while talking about students who pledged, then called his office for help after being physically beaten or threatened by the group.

"It is very frustrating for those of us who constantly hear these kind of things are going on. The victims tell us what's happened then make us promise not to tell anyone. They're embarrassed to stand up publicly and say, 'I was sexually assaulted' or 'I was beaten,' or 'I chose to be involved in this group.' There is a sentiment that once you join the organization, you are threatened if you consider leaving," he said, pausing.

"Entry into that organization is far more innocent than perhaps the outcome. They are almost trapped. I think out of thirty-five or forty members of this group, based on the allegations we have heard, there are some bad folks in there."

He called the fraternity a source of frustration for the university.

"You're talking about an individual or group that happens to be alleged suspects in a lot of things. But victim after victim refuses to really empower us to take action against that person or persons, because the alleged victim is either threatened or unwilling or unable to pursue it or empower us to pursue it. Like I said, it's really frustrating."

While driving home, I thought about the strange phone calls Jack had made to his former high school teacher and wondered if he placed the same type of calls to anyone else in the family.

"Are you sure Jack never said anything to you about his fraternity?" I said again to his mother that night, thinking she must know something.

"I do recall an incident that happened at the end of his freshman year," Elaine said, after taking a few minutes to collect her thoughts. "Jack went to a rock concert in Pittsburgh with some of his fraternity brothers. Apparently, they stole some T-shirts got caught, threw the shirts into Jack's arms, and then ran away. They arrested Jack and took him to the police station."

She posted bond.

"I told him these people are not your friends. Friends wouldn't do that to another friend. He was very upset by the entire situation."

Over the summer, they talked more about the incident and she also recalled their conversations about death.

"We wrote letters while he was at Virginia Beach and talked on the phone about death and dying. At the time, I thought it had something to do with my volunteer work with AIDS patients," she said. "I thought it was a little strange then. Now I think it's even stranger."

"Did Jack contact you often while away at school?" I said, trying to jog more memories.

"We usually talked at least once a week," she said.

"Anything stick out in your mind?" I said. "Was he still talking about death?"

"There were a few strange calls, now that I think about it. He called and asked me if I still needed him to come home over the weekend. I didn't know what he was talking about. I just knew he wanted me to say he had to come home that weekend. I thought it was very strange. The next time I talked to him I asked him about the call and he just said his fraternity brothers wanted him to go out and party and he didn't want to go. He brushed it off."

"This might be difficult, but do you remember when this happened?" I said

"I'll have to think about it," she replied.

"It's important," I told her. "If you can pinpoint a date, that'd be great."

"Did Jack's father and stepmother receive 'strange' phone calls, too?" I wondered, while pushing the buttons on the phone. Lisa picked up. I asked the same questions.

"He was good about keeping in touch and letting us know what was going on," she said. "Sometimes the calls were strange, though. Like the one time he called and asked me if this was the weekend he was supposed to drive me to the doctor's. I didn't know what he was talking about but I knew he wanted me to say it was. I got the feeling that there was someone there with him listening to his conversation. I told him he did have to come home that weekend. He asked if dad could ride me instead. I told him no. He said he would be here to take me. I even called Jack at work to tell him about the phone call and ask if I did the right thing. It really shook me up at the time."

She knew immediately Jack placed the call the weekend before he disappeared. "We had plans to go bowling with him and his girlfriend the next weekend," Lisa said. "But I called him at the last minute and told him I was sick and couldn't go. He stayed at school. I've felt so guilty for a long time. He would have come home that weekend. Instead he ended up dead."

John and Marisa also received a strange call from Jack during the same period, which meant, after Elaine reported back with a date, Jack had phoned someone each week that term to establish verifiable reasons to come home weekends.

I searched the IUP police report, looking for names of non-members that had been associated with the so-called fraternity. I contacted one girl identified as a "little sister." She refused to talk until offered anonymity. Once I reassured her, however, she talked up a storm about the weekend parties at the fraternity house.

"There were many fights," she said. "Even though I've been away from IUP for four years, I'm still afraid to talk about them. They will retaliate. I don't want involved."

"Do you think they're capable of hurting someone who wanted out?" I said, shocked as the word flew out of my mouth. I didn't expect an answer.

"There is no doubt in my mind they'd hurt someone who tried to get away from them," she said, offering the name of one member who met that fate.

"Yes, I am still scared of them and you should be, too!" she said. "That's all I want to say." Click.

Directory assistance provided a number to go with the name she offered. A woman answered and I asked for the former student by name.

"That's my son," the woman said. "Who's this?" I explained.

163

"Someone told me about your son being beaten while away at school," I said, treading softly. "How is he doing?"

"They beat him within an inch of his life!" she said, her voice turning frantic. "He was hospitalized with a ruptured spleen and other internal injuries. He's lucky to be alive!"

"Is he alright now?" I said. "Do you think he might speak…"

"No!" she snapped. "He left school and does not want to be involved in this matter any more."

Weeks later, I also discovered the names of two students who filed charges against members of Jack's fraternity listed on the court docket in the magistrate's office. I jotted down their phone numbers.

One former student said that he and his friend walked into a bar where the pseudo fraternity members already in the bar identified them as members of a rival fraternity. One of them ended up on bathroom floor with a broken jaw; the other kid was kicked and punched about the head and left for dead on the sidewalk in front of the bar in broad daylight. They both pressed charges then waited for notification of the hearing, which according to the court docket had already been held.

"This is a bunch of shit!" the kid on the phone said. "How do they get away with these things? No one even notified us about the hearing. We never heard anything! What happened?"

"They were put on probation then later their records were expunged," I said, amazed he didn't know.

"That's what they got for almost beating us to death!" he said. "Probation and no record. How's that possible?"

"I don't know," I said, wondering myself how the hearing had been held without plaintiffs.

Memorial stone purchased by Jack's fraternity brothers that now sits under a tree across from the stairwell where his body was found on the IUP campus.

(Photograph by Marlene Gentilcore)

# EIGHTEEN

*True patriotism hates injustice in its own land
more than anywhere else.*

CLARENCE SEWARD DARROW

When I called John the next day to tell him about my interview with the director of student affairs, he said, "Sounds like my brother joined a fraternity that turned out to be a gang of men—a sort of legal gang."

A few minutes later, my fellow reporter called to say she had a copy of the Indiana Borough police report in hand and had scheduled an interview with Dr. Griffin the following week. We met at the Corner Restaurant in New Alexander, halfway between Pittsburgh and Greensburg. We ordered lunch, talked about the upcoming interview, and she handed me the report. I could hardly wait to see what it said since Police Chief Antolik told John to get a subpoena.

I got home, stretched out on the living room rug with the two police reports on the floor front of me. I picked up the first page of the university police report, which stated police from the Greensburg Crime Lab examined the scene and took photographs. The IUP investigating officer called Indiana Borough police for backup and summoned IUP administrators to the stairwell. University and borough police conducted a grid search of the stairwell; no additional evidence was found.

IUP police received a phone call from the president of the Phi Delt fraternity at 12:30 a.m. to report a rumor that Jack's fraternity planned to retaliate against their fraternity because a Phi Delt member was involved in a fight with Jack prior to his disappearance.

The IUP officer met with Antolik at nine-thirty the next morning to review his investigation up to that point. According to Indiana Borough police records, Jack's fraternal big brother walked across town alone to Jack's apartment on Friday, October 16. Jack drove them two blocks to a party at the Alpha Gamma sorority house located across the street from the main entrance to IUP campus.

They left the party around eleven-thirty with three other fraternity brothers and another student. The group split into two groups of three across the street from the sorority house in front of the main campus entrance on Oakland Avenue. Three, including Jack and his big brother, took Oakland Avenue to Seventh Avenue headed towards the business district. The other three cut across campus, also ending up on Seventh Avenue where one of the group claims to have seen Jack with his entourage in front of Tom's Pizza Shop, while standing in front of the Phi Sig fraternity house some three blocks away—good eyes!

The same person also told police, when he arrived at the bar, he asked the bartender if he wanted him to check I.D.'s at the door. He said Jack was in the bar when he arrived. He didn't know if Jack had anything to drink but stated if he did someone must have bought it for him.

Jack's fraternal big brother told police he and Jack left the bar to go to his apartment so he could change his clothes. He said Jack was not intoxicated because he did not have any problem

167

walking up two flights of stairs to his apartment. Now this gets weird. He said he changed his clothes and Jack asked to wear his fraternity jacket.

This comment struck a nerve since the sorority girl I spoke to said kids made fun of Jack at the party earlier because the name on the fraternity jacket he wore wasn't his. Also, Jack's roommate explained during a phone interview that Jack's fraternal big brother gave Jack the jacket at their house at least two weeks before the sorority party. He didn't know why he gave it to him or why Jack wore it that night instead of his own.

Jack's fraternal big brother also told police a fight broke out in the bar and all the fraternity brothers went outside "to let it happen" then filed back in. Sometime later, the bartender escorted Jack to the door for fighting, "and because the victim was discovered to be under 21 years old." Eyewitnesses place Jack in the bar for around forty-five minutes.

The only non-fraternity member who left the party with Jack refused to talk to either police force without an attorney present and was never questioned again. When contacted the student said, "I don't know why everyone keeps asking me about this case. I don't know anything. I don't want to get anyone in trouble."

"Well, if you don't know anything, how can you get anyone in trouble?" would have been my next question if he hadn't hung up.

The person Jack allegedly fought with in the bar told police Jack kept asking him loudly, "Am I fucked up?"

"Everyone told me to just tell him that he is fucked up and let it go but instead I told him, 'You're double fucked up!' At this point, Jack supposedly grabbed him by his jacket. The bartender broke up the scuffle and escorted Jack to the door.

Reading both reports together filled in many blanks concerning the people and places Jack encountered on the night he disappeared, the difference being the Indiana Borough report included hand-written statements from the student who walked him back to campus and the two female students Jack encountered while walking across the street to the second bar he visited that night. Both girls said Jack came up to them complaining about being kicked out of the bar.

"He was walking with us and acting like he knew us," one of the girls wrote in her police statement. "I had seen him somewhere before so I didn't think too much of it. He asked Denise what fraternity we're in. She said we are in Caleco's. He didn't hear and asked again. I said we are in Caleco's. Then he either said, 'Gee thanks you guys, you just saved me' or 'You just saved my life.' I don't remember which one. He asked us if we wanted a beer. We said no. He walked up to the bar and got a beer. He was with a group of people when we left a few minutes later."

The words, "You just saved my life" made my flesh quiver. Did Jack know he was going to die that night and who would kill him? Is that why he kept telling everyone about terrible headaches and yelling in the bar, "Am I fucked up?" What about the strange phone calls he made looking for legitimate reasons to come home as someone on his end listened in? And, the conversations with his mother that summer about death and dying.

"I look back now, I should have known something was wrong," Elaine said during one of our conversations.

The student believed to be the last person to have seen Jack alive told me he barely knew Jack and only saw him at fraternity parties. In the police report, however, he said he knew Jack for about "one year and had been drinking with him several times." He also said, "He'd never seen Davis as intoxicated as he was on the night of October 16-17, 1987."

His words the night we spoke rang in my ears, "I've seen people a lot drunker than Jack was that night." Why did he change his story? After reading his handwritten police statement, I totally freaked out.

> "...I did not know where he lived so I tried walking him somewhat towards campus until I could find out. He tried to resist me walking him home a few times, but I was able to keep him moving. When I asked him where he lived, he told me Oakland Avenue. But as we walked he would try to resist going home again and would point in different directions, saying, 'I live that way.' I asked him again where he lived when we got in front of Elkin Hall. 'Right here, this is where I live.' I said, 'You can't live here J.D. This is a bush.' He told me to leave. I didn't have to worry about him. I told him I was still going to take him home but he was stubborn and refused to walk and he refused to tell me where he lived...I told him that if anything happens to him I would be mad at him. He said, 'Tom, if anything happens to me tonight you can kick my ass tomorrow.' He again told me to go home. I walked around a bush towards Elkin Hall. I looked back and saw Jack peeking through the bush. When he saw me look back he told me to keep going and that he would be O.K. That was the last time I saw him...I left Elkin Hall and walked to my fraternity house to spend the night."

Why was Jack hiding in the bushes?

Unlike the IUP police report, the borough police report mentions the toxicology report at the end.

"5 Jan 88—met with Coroner Tom Streams, Dr. Griffin, Indiana Hospital Pathologist, and IUP Safety Director Paul Lang at Dr. Griffin's hospital office. We went over the toxicology report of blood, urine, and gastric samples. Blood alcohol level would have been no lower than .158 before death. Blood was in a jelly like stage, indicating the body had undergone a number of warm up and cool down cycles over a number of days. The lack of alcohol in the blood is probably due to the fact that the white and red corpuscles metabolized the alcohol as these corpuscles live for several hours after death. In the doctor's opinion, it is possible that Davis lived for an hour or two after having reached the bottom of the stairwell. There were no indications of recent cocaine or marijuana usage. The trace found were probably from at least a week prior to death. Dr. Griffin stated that no information contained in this report would cause a change in the original autopsy report as to cause of death."

There it was in black and white, Officer Antolik included Dr. Griffin's explanation about the body continuing to function after death in his report.

"That's like saying a person can still see with their eyes after they are dead," Dr. Charles Winek, director and chief toxicologist at the Allegheny County Criminal Laboratory in Pittsburgh said during an interview in his office one afternoon. "A medical doctor said these things? Any seventh grade biology student can tell you the body does not continue to function after death. When you're dead—you're dead—your body stops functioning! Your heart stops beating, it stops pumping blood through the veins and the liver cannot function to metabolize anything. Your body stops functioning, period."

He also called the alcohol findings in the toxicology report strange. "There is no explanation for the alcohol. If there is alcohol in the urine then it should be in the blood. The amount in the stomach is puzzling. The temperature at the time suggests there should not be any fermentation. It is such a small amount of alcohol, not even two ounces of beer. Can't say it is not impossible that it is not fermentation. Usually, however, if there is fermentation, you find it in the blood because of the de-fusion."

He shook his head as he spoke, "The stupid part of this is once you're dead, once you stop breathing and your heart stops beating—you're dead—you're pronounced dead. That doesn't mean everything stops immediately, but alcohol does not continue to metabolize after death. That's impossible because the site for that to occur is the liver, and if the heart is not pumping blood, the blood that is in your heart and throughout your body can't possibly move to be metabolized. The blood has to go to the liver and the pump that gets it there isn't working anymore. Metabolism after death does not occur. I think that's simple. The liver is the major site of metabolism for everything. No alcohol in the blood means there was none there at the time the person died."

He also offered another possible explanation for the strange alcohol results; perhaps the person took a couple swigs of beer then instantly dropped dead. Now I understood why the lab tested for "sudden death." And also wondered, although no one mentioned it, if a more sinister scenario existed? Did someone try to pour alcohol down his throat after death?"

Think about it. Could the tiny amount of alcohol actually found have trickled down into his stomach, but with no bodily functions, never metabolize into his blood? As for the urine, the scant amount is insignificant. Perhaps the remnants of beer he drank twenty-four hours before his demise that had not been completely eliminated from his system? Makes you wonder after hearing twice from two different sources on separate occasions that someone vomited in his mouth after death.

That night, my imagination ran wild as soon as my eyes closed hoping for sleep. I kept seeing Jack peeking through the bushes and sneaking around in the dark trying to save his own life. The mere thought that he might have known he was going to die made me sick. As a matter of fact, I got so freaked out; I jumped out of bed, pulled on some clothes, ran out of my apartment in the middle of the night, and drove away.

I didn't know where I was going. I just knew I desperately needed to get away from it all. I took an interstate ramp headed south to West Virginia. The possibility that Jack might have been hunted down and murdered in cold blood was more than I could stand. After working on this case day and night for two months twenty-four/seven, I needed to run away and drove as far as my tired body could take me. I ended up calling my doctor from a phone in some cheap, dinky motel to explain the situation and ask her to call the nearest pharmacy to prescribe something to calm me down then gave her the number.

Mentally and physically exhausted, I slept on and off for the next three days. Woke up, got something to eat, came back, fell right back to sleep. I didn't want to think about it anymore and shut the investigation out of my mind.

The description of Jack hiding in the bushes and his words, "You just saved my life" combined with the strange phone calls home prior to his death painted a picture too gruesome to contemplate with or without rose-colored glasses.

# NINETEEN

*To see what is right and not do it is want of courage.*

Confucius

After a much-needed rest, I was back on the job. Conducting an investigation is like building a jigsaw puzzle; you have to recognize, organize and sort out details in order to fit pieces together to form a complete picture. Unlike store-bought puzzles, however, there's no complete image on the front of the box to glance at when stuck with a piece that doesn't seem to fit no matter how hard you force it. You also have to collect your own pieces by asking questions and doing research. The hard part is figuring out whether pieces do or do not fit as you strive to construct the truest image.

I drew up a list of questions a few days before the scheduled interview with Dr. Griffin, which Coroner Streams decided to attend. Jack's blood alcohol level was number one.

"You have to take into consideration the circumstances," Dr. Griffin said. "A gelatinous material was sent to the lab. It came back not detected because of the state of the blood."

"So, how would his death be called, 'alcohol-related' if there was no alcohol in the blood?" my fellow reporter asked.

"She's as cool as a cucumber," I thought, listening to the tape, grateful she conducted the interview instead of me.

"That was not determined," Dr. Griffin said. "The amounts in the stomach and urine were small. That's how we determined, because it was there, alcohol related. It is possible that he was in the stairwell some time before he vomited. That's possible. He was debilitated by some manner, alcohol or some other manner. We couldn't find an absolute level of any material to determine why he was debilitated. These levels could not be determined because of the state of the body when it was found."

I recalled Dr. Wecht's words that Jack could not have been dead for more than twenty-four hours due to this body being in a state of rigor mortis when found.

"We can't tell from the toxicology report why he aspirated his stomach contents," Dr. Griffin said.

"This is the family's biggest problem," the reporter said. "You say this death is alcohol-related but there is no evidence that backs up this theory. Is there other reasons why he would aspirate his own vomit?"

"My personal theory is he walked down there to urinate, slumped down the wall unconscious and vomited. The position of his legs shows he did not fall down there. He walked down," Coroner Streams said. "The county coroner investigates only to the point that it was an accident, homicide, or suicide. It is not my job to determine the manner of death. We took this case much further. First, we determined it was an accident and not an act by another person; that is the county code. All we determine is the manner of death, not the cause of death. The evidence in this case is theorized that this happened. Can we document or prove it? No. We know it wasn't a homicide; we know that he wasn't hit over the head and thrown down there."

What made him so sure? I thought. How did he know?

175

"No, I didn't open his skull," Dr. Griffin said. "The outside didn't show any evidence of trauma. Would it be routine? No. It depends on what you see and the circumstances. I saw no reason to examine it in this case."

She flowed from one question to the next without skipping a beat, a professional on a fact-finding mission, "Why did it take almost three months to get the toxicology report back from the lab?"

"The delay was because the results were lost in the mail," Dr. Griffin said.

I've often wondered what Streams thought at that moment. He read the correspondence between Dr. Griffin and Roche Laboratories; he handed them to John. He knew the toxicology report was not lost in the mail.

"You know there are controlled substances involved here," Dr. Griffin said.

Like Streams, he played the drug card, despite his own words in the autopsy addendum, "certain drugs of abuse were identified. However, the levels of these substances do not indicate a significant role in demise."

"We are all concerned here," Coroner Streams said towards the end of the interview. "We've seen enough *20/20* and *60 Minutes* to realize something like this is being investigated. A public exposition is not the best route to take, especially if someone is involved in this death."

I rewound the tape. Didn't Streams just say a few minutes ago, "We know it wasn't homicide..."

The next day, the editors were ready to run the story. My co-worker and I agreed, she'd write the story; I'd feed her the facts. At this point, my objectivity was questionable at best. I felt drained, exhausted, overwhelmed and doubted my own ability to turn the important facts of this case into a concise, interesting and readable news story.

I didn't sleep at all waiting for the paper to hit newsstands early that Sunday morning. I drove to the local convenience store and back several times, anxious for delivery. Right before daybreak, the big stack of papers arrived with my story splashed across the front page!

The first of part of the three-part series, *"Death on Campus"* ran on April 29, 1990. The headline read, *"IUP student's 1987 death still troubles family"* with Jack's high school portrait to the right of the copy. The in-depth article provided background information and listed the "troubling circumstances" surrounding his death.

> Item – If Jack Davis' death was alcohol related, why do toxicology tests show only small amounts of alcohol in his stomach and urine? More curious is the amount of alcohol found in the blood. Toxicology results: "None detected."
>
> Item – According to forensic experts, in order to aspirate enough stomach contents to fill the "bronchial tree" and asphyxiate, the victim first must have been unconscious. The Indiana Hospital pathologist who performed the autopsy concedes nothing in the toxicology report or autopsy findings indicates why Davis was unconscious.
>
> Item – According to Indiana County Coroner Thomas Streams, the body lay at the bottom of the stairwell for nearly five days. The victim's family, desperate to find their missing son, asked Indiana Borough police to search campus grounds. They were turned down. Only after family members organized their own search

> party did police agree to participate. Davis' body was found less than a half hour later.
>
> Item – The victim's family, told a fraternity fight occurred the night Jack was last seen, suspected he had been fatally injured. They said their suspicions were reinforced after some of Jack's fraternity brothers showed up at the funeral with blackened eyes, cuts and bruises. IUP officials described the alleged fraternity fight as a "shouting match."

Personal background information about the family was included as well as an overview of the original autopsy findings, the toxicology results and Streams' theory.

> "I could have believed Jack got drunk and even choked on his vomit, but the way they said it happened doesn't make sense," Jack Davis, Sr. said. "He never would have walked down 21 steps to urinate. I know my son. He would've just gone down far enough to where he couldn't be seen. Why would he walk all the way to the bottom of that stairwell?"
>
> Streams said he based his 'alcohol-related' conclusion on information given to borough police by IUP student Tom Brennan. Brennan said he met up with Davis in downtown Indiana at 1 a.m. Saturday, Oct. 17.
>
> "He was very drunk," Brennan said. "He was using the wall to hold himself up. I told him to come to my house, which was nearby, but he didn't want to."

As I read his comments, I wondered why he described Jack as "not falling down drunk" during our phone conversation. Did he just say that because I was investigating for the family and he wanted to make them feel better?

"About 10 minutes before we got to Elkin, J.D. (Jack Davis) went to the bathroom right near somebody's house," Brennan said. "He wasn't at all shy about it. Later when the body was found, I couldn't figure out why he would've walked all the way to the bottom of the stairwell. It didn't make sense."

The last two sentences in the article read:

*Why was Jack Davis unconscious? Griffin concedes nothing in the autopsy or subsequent toxicology tests provide the answer.*

I let out a huge sigh of relief. It was over, or so I thought.

John called, frantic; the media blitz was on.

"You have to be here!" he said, panic-stricken. "I don't know what to say to these people."

"You can meet them here in my apartment," I said, half asleep.

Shortly after noon, cameras rolled. John sat at the small round table in my tiny dining area; I stood in the doorway of the kitchen, inches behind the cameraman. Reporters asked questions. John looked at me and I whispered or mouthed the answers.

"Who are you?" one reporter finally turned around and said. I explained and within seconds ended up sitting across the table from John. There's nothing like making your television debut after being up all night. Never mind the fact that I hadn't washed my hair for several days, maybe even a week—it wasn't even combed! Regardless, there we were headlining the six o'clock news on all three major Pittsburgh stations.

The very next day, Monday, April 30, the front-page headline read: *"Findings disputed in student's death."* The second part of the series rehashed and raised questions about the results of the toxicology report.

Dr. James Frost, medical examiner for the state of West Virginia and Dr. Katherine Jasnosz, a forensic pathologist with the Allegheny County Coroner's office went head-to-head with Coroner Streams and Dr. Griffin.

Coroner Streams and Dr. Griffin stood by their findings; Dr. Frost and Dr. Jasnosz tore them apart.

> Frost, who is also an inspector with the National Association for Medical Examiners, said the unanswered forensic questions regarding Davis' death are serious.
>
> "If I were investigating this office for accreditation and this case were given to me for review," Frost said emphatically. "I'd flunk 'em. And I'd want to see how they handled other forensic cases."

The last two lines in the article read:

> After reviewing the autopsy report and toxicology reports, does Frost know how Jack Davis died?
>
> "No clue," Frost said. "This investigation never should have been closed."

Coroner Streams was pictured to the right of the copy with a concerned look on his face.

The proverbial shit hit the fan! Reporters crawled all over Indiana and hounded the family for comments.

The three-part series ended Tuesday, May 1 with Jack's high school portrait next to a picture of Elaine and Jack Sr. looking through a family photo album on the front page above the headline, *"Parents recall agonizing search for son."*

Details of his death are explained, then Elaine, Jack Sr. and Jack's brother Mike, recall their search for Jack, and Indiana Borough Detective Antolik defends his decision not to conduct a search.

He said with the amount of foot traffic on campus and with IUP work crews constantly about, he never suspected the victim was on university grounds.

> "When the body was found on campus, it astonished me," Antolik said. "With the amount of time that had passed since he was last seen, I thought he probably had been kidnapped."

Antolik further said he assumed IUP checked all campus stairwells regularly.

The final article ended with a quote from John.

> "I'm working two jobs right now to get attorney fees together," John Lynch said. "If I have to work night and day, I'll do it. I'll never give up until I know what really happened. Never."

Local newscasts featured follow-up stories for several weeks; articles ran almost daily in all three major newspapers. In one article, IUP police threatened to arrest me for posing as the victim's sister to obtain information and documents. The editor called to ask if this was true. I assured him I never identified myself as Jack's sister, only as someone looking into his death for the family. I explained John told Streams I was his sister the day he picked up the toxicology report. I was not there.

Family members called day and night to keep me up to speed, ask questions or ask for answers to questions for the press. I found myself in the middle of something I never saw coming.

Questions about exhuming Jack's body made headlines. The media push was on. Dr. Wecht took center stage. Never in my wildest dreams did I expect all the hoopla.

I didn't miss an afternoon or evening newscast for weeks. The cat and dog fight between Coroner Streams and Dr. Wecht was in full swing, fur flying in all directions. I watched amazed by the passionate reaction my investigation invoked in so many people.

About a month later, the media hype faded to a mere whisper, which suited me just fine. I needed a rest and slept as much as possible, taking naps just about every day to catch up on many sleepless nights. One afternoon, I fell asleep and into a dream I'll never ever forget.

I was walking with Jack cradled in my arms as if he were a baby. He appeared healthy and whole with no blood anywhere. He pointed up towards the sky, which was not blue; instead pure white like the light that surrounded us. He kept pointing up, explaining something as if giving me directions. I was nodding and smiling, understanding completely. Then all of a sudden, I lifted his full-grown body, which was as light as a feather, straight up into the air. *WHOOSH!* He was gone.

In the exact same instant, my body felt as if every drop of energy was sucked with great force out of my body up toward the ceiling, as I lay sprawled out on the bed. *ZAP!* My eyes snapped open. I couldn't move a muscle, my entire body as limp as a rag doll—a terrified trembling, rag doll to be exact. I stared at the ceiling, waiting to recover enough strength to move. I felt completely different, calm, serene, but shaken.

A few hours later, I borrowed money from my mom, packed a bag, and drove to Atlantic City to clear my head. I needed to escape for a while and playing Blackjack for money takes your mind off everything. I stayed five days walked by the ocean and won a little extra cash, which came in handy. I had no money and my future at the paper looked grim. Funny, the repercussions and consequences of investigating this case had never crossed my mind as I set off in search of the truth.

Somewhere in the back of my idealistic and naive mind, I believed once the truth got out, proper public officials, law enforcement or someone—anyone—would examine the facts, reopen the case immediately and justice would prevail.

If you wear rose-colored glasses, you have to learn to deal with disappointment and frustration, and constantly struggle with acceptance. The media went home but family members kept in touch to tell me about the strangers who called wanting to share their own tragic stories or offer information about Jack's death.

"He was in the wrong place at the wrong time wearing the wrong jacket," one person told John. Another told Marisa her daughter was with Jack when he died but refused to leave a name or number.

"He was carried into the stairwell on Wednesday morning," was a message left on their answering machine; again, no contact information.

The paper also received calls.

One student said she was told someone vomited in Jack's mouth to make it look like he choked to death. Another said he used the stairwell as a short cut to class during the five days in question and no body was there. No names no numbers. It got old real fast.

Around the end of September, I set up an appointment to talk with my co-worker about writing a second series of articles for the paper.

"I can't work with you on this story anymore," she said, as we sat in the lunchroom again. No expression on her face as she dropped a bomb.

"What's the matter?" I said. "They don't want to do it?"

"I've been told that you have been getting drugs as payment from a member of the family to investigate Jack's death," she said. "I do not feel comfortable working with you anymore."

"What!" flew out of my mouth. "Why are you saying these things?"

She explained a reporter in her office told the editor who told her. I couldn't believe it. Apparently, my co-worker in the Pittsburgh office, the "friend" who stopped by for a few beers during the investigation, was the one who started the rumor. I was stunned! Why would he say such a thing? Why did he want to ruin my reputation?

"And you believe this about me?" I said, staring in her face, insulted and pissed. No response. I stood, walked straight through the newsroom and out the door. I drove home, confused and devastated but mindful enough to contact a lawyer the minute I reached my front door.

As directed, I sent a letter to the editor demanding the reporter explain and apologize for his accusations within five days or legal action would be taken against all parties concerned. The deadline was met but the situation did not end there.

"If you're a friend of hers you better tell her to get off this story or she will not be working here much longer," the editor told the same co-worker "friend" in his office a few days later.

At least now I understood, the paper did not want to deal with this story. And the thought of losing my job scared the hell out of me. I had bills to pay. So, a day after receiving the message, I met with the editor in his office and promised to stop. He said people in Indiana were angry and Coroner Streams threatened not to speak to their reporters ever again. He also told me I was not a good writer.

"Come with me," he said standing up, then walked around his desk with his arm outstretched to usher me in the right direction. "I want this to end right here and now."

He made a beeline for my fellow reporter's desk; she glanced up from her computer screen with a blank look on her face.

"There will be no more written about this unless Wecht exhumes the body," he said sternly. "Do you both understand?"

Her face turned red from the neck up; we both nodded. I left the building with a huge lesson about the media and people in general tucked neatly under my belt. Later that night, I told John what happened over the phone.

"Screw them!" he said, going into red-face mode. "They think someone in this family gave you drugs to investigate Jack's death? Is that what they said? Is that what they think of you after all your hard work? Is that what they think of us? I can't believe it! All we want to know is the truth, assholes!"

"They said no more stories unless Wecht exhumes the body," I said, hearing extreme pain and deep sorrow in my own voice.

# TWENTY

*Without justice, courage is weak.*
           Benjamin Franklin

The Indiana County district attorney held all the power now. He evaluated new evidence, decided whether an investigation was warranted, then agreed or not to foot the bill to exhume the body for a second autopsy.

"Why don't you just ask him, John?" I said on the phone that night. "All he can say is no."

John and Marisa met with him a week later to plead their case.

"You're not going to believe this," Marisa said, calling me the minute they got home. "The district attorney agreed to reopen the investigation. I can't believe it!"

"That's wonderful," I said. "I can't believe it either."

"No publicity," John said when Marisa handed him the phone. "He wants to keep it quiet." Long pause. "It sounds like they might just want to shut us up and sweep it all under the rug like they did before."

"Why don't you call him and ask him why he wants to keep this quiet," I said, sensing he was fishing for an opinion.

The D.A. told him it would be better if it was kept quiet but if John wanted to go to the media, it was up to him. He didn't care either way.

John contacted the *Tribune*; the story ran the next day.

"Our office wasn't involved in the original investigation because it was labeled an accidental death," Martin said. "But Dr. Wecht has told me there are aspects about the autopsy and pathological findings that just don't jive. I have a hell of a lot of respect for Dr. Wecht... This is not like a retail theft where I might say the police investigation is good enough for me. We have a person who lost his life. If he died under circumstances other than the official ruling, I want to know about it."

The family, totally elated, soaked up the D.A.'s words like dry sponges. Finally, someone in power had promised to get to the bottom of Jack's death. The first real hope they had in years. Too bad it ended so soon. Two days later, the D.A. suspended the investigation "because of the publicity generated by the family, which may have compromised a probe."

His unexpected move shocked everyone, including Dr. Wecht.

"Either a second look is merited or it is not," he told reporters. "People are going to find out about the investigation anyway. After person A is interviewed, he is naturally going to tell B through Z. People do talk to each other. I don't understand this."

Angry, John told the press he was going to drive to the state attorney general's office if he had to, in order to get someone to investigate his brother's death. The D.A.'s decision generated more flack than even he probably imagined. Sympathy for the family hit an all-time high; the outraged public saw the D.A.'s turnabout as another slap in face of Jack's grieving parents. This was probably not the publicity the Indiana County D.A. and candidate for common pleas court judge planned to generate a month before elections.

In an editorial, the *Tribune-Review* called for an end of the suspension quoting the D.A.'s own words, "If, as it has been suggested, Davis may have been the victim of foul play, it would be immoral not to reopen this case."

When asked, Coroner Streams said he had no intention of reopening the case. The local news ate it all up.

"We just got a call from *Pittsburgh's Talking*," Marisa said, excited. "They want the family to be on the show."

The morning program aired two days later with Elaine, Jack Sr. and John center stage. I politely refused to participate in the broadcast, preferring to brief John, write questions and answers, and then sit back in the audience to watch the drama unfold.

The host, Ann Devlin, provided background information and asked the family questions during the first part of the show. Then, Dr. Wecht joined the panel the second half to discuss and dispute the toxicology report, other forensic evidence, as well as the original autopsy and the Indiana County coroner's theory.

No one from Indiana appeared on the show; instead the university and Coroner Streams sent statements the host read on air. IUP President John D. Welty said they continue to sympathize with the family and promised full cooperation. The coroner promised to reopen the case if new evidence was presented.

"This is the first I've heard. We're happy to hear these things," Elaine said before John interrupted.

"That's what they say now, but no one's been very cooperative so far."

I smiled watching, grateful for the family's chance to speak out and take a stand with an expert at their side. Dr. Wecht presented many interesting facts, however, the most memorable segment of the show came at the end when the host took calls from viewers.

Everyone in the studio, including the host, looked confused by the hostility of the first few callers, who pounced on the family because they didn't like the way the town of Indiana was being portrayed. Others, in so many words, told them to move on, accept their son's fate and be grateful they found his body. In response to Dr. Wecht explaining Jack's three-day beard growth and asking anyone with information to contact the station, one girl reported seeing Jack the night he disappeared and verified he was clean-shaven.

"We have time for one more call," the host said, "Caller are you there?"

"I just want to say I've seen what goes on in Indiana County. There is so much corruption in this county, and if you're not part of it but you know what's going on, or are a snitch, you're in big trouble," the woman said, making everyone wince, even the host.

"This is not the only unsolved death here. There are lots of them here, and if you don't just let it go you're in big trouble. The corruption includes high officials in the county and if this family is dealing with the officials in this county they aren't going to uncover anything."

John stared at me, wide-eyed, his head moving slowly from side to side. Elaine and Jack Sr. fidgeted in their seats, not sure where to look or what to do. The host looked up, head tilted, listening with the same quizzical look on her face as most of the audience.

"I know a lot of people who are under threats on account of things like this. People are moved out or paid off."

"What exactly are we talking about here?" the host finally asked, befuddled.

"The drug industry is massive in this county. They are involved in the transportation, distribution, manufacturing, and sale of drugs. It's not just this county; they are all tied together in this industry. The only way to survive in this county is to keep your mouth shut. When you find out what is going on here and they know you know, you might as well forget it."

"You're not keeping your mouth shut," the host said with a confrontational tone of voice. "It sure sounds like you're speaking up."

"Well," the caller said. "I've written letters but nobody does nothing about it anyway." She did not leave her name.

After taking a few more questions from the audience, the show ended. We went home. In the days that followed, the family received phone calls and a few letters, among them one written by a student entitled *"Taking a Stand for Jack"*, published in the university's student paper, *The Penn*.

> Sometimes it seems so long ago—Oct. 21, 1987. Now we are all reliving it again. So Jack, this one is from me to you. We all miss you.
>
> I would like to address everyone who thinks that the investigation of Jack Allan Davis, Jr. is a toy with which to play. The fact that Jack's case has taken this long to be re-opened in the first place is pitiful. What really tops it all is that now that there is publicity surrounding the case, the district attorney's office wants to suspend it. I would like to know if D.A. William Martin understands what he is doing to the feelings of all the people involved who knew Jack. It is hard enough for Jack's family and friends to go through all the pain again, let alone having him decide to throw in a suspension.

*What does this "suspension" mean, exactly? That no one can do this or their job now?*

*Why is it that no one with authority wants to get to the bottom of this case? I would like to inform all the "professionals" in this case that all this dodging is not making any of you look good. In fact, you know what it looks like to all of us who knew Jack? A cover up. So, let's stop fooling around with this case. Jack is gone. The least we can do for him now is to get to the truth, because everyone who knew Jack knows that this was no accident.*

*The last person(s) I would like to address is whoever is responsible for Jack's death. I'm sure in the past almost three years the person(s) at fault have felt a big relief, as if they're off the hook. But guess what? It's time and I hope that you are scared, because you should be; justice will be served, it is judgment day. I would like to thank "The Penn" for its editorial 'Open & Shut Case.' I'm glad someone else can see the point of view of the people who cared for Jack."*

Kathleen Gillette

The Penn also printed an article entitled, "Articles disputed, case remains closed," which stated the university had no plans to reopen the investigation because "the doubts raised deal with a difference of opinion between pathologists." Their opinions were cited from articles printed in the *Tribune* in which Frost states the death should never have been ruled alcohol-related even though alcohol was found in the stomach and urine and Streams disagreed.

*Streams said just because the toxicology tests show no alcohol in the bloodstream, it does not mean it was* not there. "It just means the condition of the body was such that the alcohol was undetectable," he said.

Streams said as far as he is concerned the Davis case is closed.

"I cannot say what caused Jack Davis to become unconscious, but I can say that he was not thrown over that railing or hit on the head and dumped there," he said.

"We have assumed that there had to be alcohol though because it was found in sufficient levels in his stomach," Streams added.

He said marijuana and cocaine were also found in Davis' system, but that was released by the family not him.

"I tried to save them some grief by not releasing that, but the family themselves brought it up in the articles."

Streams said he felt the series of articles were biased and sensationalized.

He said one of the reporters obtained a copy of the toxicology report by telling him she was Davis' sister. Streams said he did not find out until several days later that she was not a family member.

As stated in a previous chapter, John and his brother Mike went to his office to pick up the report during our first trip to Indiana while my daughter and I went to the library to do research. Streams asked John who the lady was that called him. John replied, "She's my sister, what's it to you."

Streams also sent an invoice to the *Tribune-Review* for "documents rendered from the Indiana County Coroner: Autopsy Report, $100; Toxicology Reports, $50; Coroner's Report,

$50; Death Certificate, $10." A total of $210 for documents he personally handed John.

Two weeks after closing the investigation, the Indiana County D.A. met with Dr. Wecht, reviewed new evidence, reopened the case, appointed a task force and announced, "exhumation of the body was a strong possibility."

"It's great!" John told reporters. "We support it a thousand percent. I hope it's done right and we get our fair shake."

The next day, Streams told reporters Jack's death was caused by alcohol and cocaine abuse and attributed the statement to Dr. Wecht.

"I don't understand why he is making remarks like this. I am disturbed by his apparent psychological need to go to this extent," Wecht responded, calling Streams' remarks "senseless."

A week before local elections on November 8, 1990, an Allegheny County common pleas judge granted the Indiana County district attorney permission to exhume Jack's body for a second autopsy.

"If we do find there was a blow to the head or neck severe enough to cause death that would be indicative of foul play," he told reporters. "Anytime you hear that several people refused to talk to police about Davis, you become suspicious of what they are afraid of."

Of course, there is a huge difference between dreaming and living in the reality of that dream—-perhaps nightmare is more appropriate in this case—once the dream comes true. The mere thought of Jack being dug out of the ground three years after his death shook us all up. Imagining what his decomposed body might look like when they opened the casket gave me the creeps.

"They said one of us has to identify the body," Marisa whispered on the phone the night before the exhumation. "Will you do it for us? I don't think any of us can handle it."

"What?" I said, not volunteering for this one. "That makes no sense! It's his casket, who else would be in it?"

Apparently, the D.A. told them it was a requirement. Knowing what I'd been through over the past ten months—and this family suffered a thousand times more—I couldn't imagine one of them standing in front of the pried open casket staring at the unthinkable. If I didn't do it, who would? Would I recognize him? Panicked, I called Dr. Wecht.

"Who told them that crap?" he said. "No one has to identify his body. We all know who is in the casket for God's sake. They are just trying to scare these poor people."

I felt relief mixed with disgust but my voice sounded as pleasant as pie when I called Marisa back to ease their minds, if at all possible at the time.

"This just isn't fair," Jack's sisters cried, as they watched a gigantic crane haul their brother's casket out of ground with chains on the evening news.

Dr. Wecht performed the second autopsy at St. Francis Hospital on November 13, 1990. Coroner Streams attended and videotaped the procedure. At the request of the Indiana County district attorney, Dr. Wecht did not release his findings until in front of cameras at a press conference five days later.

Unfortunately, the results leaked to the press before he told the family. Most learned Jack "died of a brain hemorrhage resulting from three skull fractures" on television. John heard the news from reporters who tracked him down at work for comment.

I often wondered why the D.A. wanted to wait five days to release the findings of the second autopsy. Who knows? What was important is the family knew the truth as they buried their loved one a second time.

# TWENTY-ONE

*One man with courage makes a majority.*

Andrew Jackson

Lights, cameras and action surrounded us as we walked into the conference room of the Hyatt Regency Hotel in downtown Pittsburgh for a press conference on Saturday, November 18, 1990. Dr. Wecht met privately with Elaine, Jack Sr. and John to discuss his findings an hour before the media event. We hooked up afterwards and walked into the large room together. They took seats up front; I sat further back.

The reporter who worked on the story with me came in and sat down next to me as if nothing happened between us. I wore my professional hat that day; we exchanged pleasantries and not much else.

"I'm going to get someone to take our picture for the cover of our book," she said before heading to find a photographer she knew from the paper. I posed for the camera, smiling while thinking this woman's nuts! I nodded and played along; she still served as the family's main media outlet and loved getting the inside scoop, which worked for me. Write a book, with her, after she insulted my integrity without question based on rumor? Was she kidding?

Dr. Wecht sat next to Indiana County D.A. William J. Martin at a table cluttered with microphones and wires at the front of the room. Dr. Wecht described in detail the three skull fractures and brain hemorrhage that caused Jack's death. Then he continued with a statement that shocked me senseless.

"The injuries are more consistent with a fall than with blows," he announced. "But how did the fall occur, that is another matter."

Martin labeled his death "suspicious" and said, "a priority in this investigation is determining where Davis died and whether he fell accidentally or was pushed."

I wanted to scream, "What the hell are you saying!" I couldn't believe my ears. No one ever believed Jack fell down those steps—not even Coroner Streams! How did he fall down fifteen steps across a ten-foot landing, down five more steps and end up slouched against the wall in the bottom of the stairwell?

"NO!" I thought, tears stinging in my eyes.

Dr. Wecht also announced Jack's organs were missing, not buried with his body, "After the first autopsy, the organs should have been put in a plastic bag and placed back in the body, but they weren't."

Streams said they were sent to the funeral home with his body but when contacted later the funeral director said no organs came with the body.

So, where did they go? How exactly do you misplace someone's internal organs? Were his liver, lungs, kidneys, spleen, intestines, gall bladder and the rest cut out of his body then carelessly left lying around the Indiana Hospital morgue? Then what? A cleaning lady came in, scooped them up in a plastic bag and tossed them in the trash?

As soon as the press conference ended, I raced to the front of the room to talk to Dr. Wecht. "How could you say he fell into that stairwell?" I said, visibly upset. "There were no cuts or bruises on his body."

"That's right. There were no bruises or lacerations on his body. He couldn't have fallen down those stairs," the doctor said. "I didn't say he fell. I said the fractures were consistent with a fall. He could have been pushed up against a flat surface such as a wall or the ground—hard—and had the same injury."

He asked me to stand up against the wall and demonstrated gently pushing my head against the wall. I walked out of the room thinking, "Why didn't you say that on camera?"

"Please ask Marisa to get me a copy of the autopsy report," I said to John as we crossed the parking lot to our cars.

The family looked as drained as I felt. We didn't speak again until Thanksgiving Day. John called, in a rage, after a man left a threatening message on his answering machine. He played it for me. I told him to call police. I called the paper.

The next day, the threat ran in the *Tribune* word for word, minus the cuss words of course.

> "I hope you are having a happy Thanksgiving pal. This is a concerned Indiana person. Why don't you leave the guy dead, already? You hurt many families including mine with this shit. You have really some fucking nerve. I hope you're satisfied. I'm fucking pissed off. I'm not giving you my number or my name, but I'm calling back. You're asking for it. You're hurting my family and you almost killed my fucking father."

John turned the tape over to Penn Hills police, sent a copy to the Indiana County district attorney and told reporters the threat didn't change anything. In fact, it made him even more determined to find the truth.

A few days later, Penn Hills police said they knew who placed the call. Coroner Streams told the Indiana County D.A. his 17-year-old son was drunk and called John's house on Thanksgiving Day because he was upset. Streams apologized publicly in all the papers. Police advised John not to press charges based on one phone call. Later we learned Streams suffered a heart attack before the holiday.

"I hope Streams drops dead," John said. "Marisa is afraid to send the kids out to play in the yard because of his son." The threat set us all on edge; we became more vigilant.

Marisa handed me a copy of the second autopsy report around the end of January 1991. I read through the document several times, looking up words in my medical dictionary. To help me visualize Jack's injuries, I drew front and back views of a skull, and then sketched in each fracture line to specification.

A three-inch fracture up the back starting at the base of his skull, a one-inch fracture above his left ear, another one-inch fracture behind his nose inside the sinus cavity, plus a major blood hemorrhage covering the right side of the brain down into the spinal cord. I tried to picture how he would have had to fall in order to crack his skull on three different sides. There had to be three major points of impact, one on the back, side and front of his head. There were no other bruises or lacerations on the body, except a minor cut above his left eye.

How did his head hit three times at different angles hard enough to crack his skull but have no other impact on the rest of his body? Can just falling down cement steps create three skull fractures on different sides of the head? How did he fall down fifteen steps, clear the ten-foot landing and continue down five more steps to the bottom? If he tumbled there'd be bruises everywhere and he'd have to be rolling pretty darn fast to roll across the ten-foot landing in the middle to get to the bottom.

Baffled, I called Carnegie Mellon University looking for answers. A physics professor concluded that the person would have to be airborne over the top of the stairwell going at least ninety miles an hour then land on his head at the bottom. That would explain the lack of bruises and largest skull fracture but not the two smaller ones. I had to call Dr. Wecht.

"I've been trying to figure this all out," I told him. "I've read your report, drawn pictures and still can't figure out how he could have fallen into that stairwell and end up with these fractures. Can you give me a possible scenario? I mean can you sort of tell me how you see him falling into the stairwell and landing on all sides of his head and face?"

"He couldn't have fallen down those steps. There were no bruises or lacerations," he said. "It is more likely that he was hit in the face with a fist—hard—or a blackjack or the butt of a gun and knocked backwards on a hard surface."

I called the paper and the story ran in the *Tribune* the next day.

In February, I twisted my ankle while walking down a flight of stairs in high-heeled shoes. I hobbled around on crutches with what felt like a one-ton cast on my right leg. Talk about frustration! Maneuvering up two flights of stairs to my second floor apartment proved no easy task and getting to assigned meetings to write stories for the paper became an even bigger challenge.

I asked to borrow a laptop computer to use during my recovery; request denied. About a week later, the editor sent a memo to the Pittsburgh office stating my rate per story was cut to the original amount paid eight years ago when I started. As they say, the writing was on the wall. I started looking for another job as soon as the cast came off my leg.

"Are you sitting down?" my fellow reporter said, so excited I thought she'd jump through the phone line. "You better sit down for this one. Are you ready?"

"Yes, I'm ready. What is it?"

"We won!" she yelled. "We won the Pennsylvania Keystone Press Award for investigative reporting!"

"Really?" I said. "What's that?"

"It's the highest award in the state," she joyfully ranted. "We'll have to go to Harrisburg to get the award, the *Tribune* will pay for everything. Are you ready to celebrate?"

Hell, I didn't even know we were nominated for an award. Sure, let's celebrate! I borrowed twenty dollars—I didn't have enough money to celebrate anything—from my boyfriend, who sat on the couch listening to our conversation. We were about to head out to dinner when the phone rang. He handed me the money and sent me off with a kiss to celebrate in Greensburg.

We met at a bar and tossed back several drinks called "Snake Bites," which I found ironically appropriate considering the circumstances. I tried to forget and forgive as we talked about winning the award, the story and other nonsense but did not feel comfortable around her. She invited me to spend the night at her place instead of driving back to Pittsburgh. I agreed out of necessity but couldn't sleep a wink, anger oozing out of every pore.

She betrayed me! Stabbed me in the back! Not even winning an award could soothe the hurt. I quietly got up before dawn and tiptoed out the door. We stayed in touch for one reason and one reason only; she provided quick access to media coverage.

A few days later, the editor asked me to come to the main office to have my picture taken. He offered his congratulations and explained the paper would pay my expenses to Harrisburg to receive the award.

"Thank you," I said, turning to walk out the door.

"Do you know how much this story cost us?" he said, through clenched teeth. "This has cost over $5,000 already!"

I smiled as the photographer snapped our picture for the Sunday edition. I lost respect for many people during this incredible journey and learned several lessons about trust, life, and myself in general.

I turned down an invitation to ride to Harrisburg with my fellow reporter and a photographer who also received the award. The thought of spending at least six hours in a car with her to and from the state capital felt unbearable. However, in an effort to appear congenial, I agreed to meet them halfway for lunch despite an extremely upset stomach and sore ankle. The doctor removed the cast on my leg a few days prior to the event.

"When do you want to get together to work on the rest of the story?" my fellow reporter said casually as we sat in a restaurant off the Pennsylvania Turnpike halfway between Pittsburgh and Harrisburg.

I stared, fork in mid-air; my eyebrows shot up, startled by her words.

"I don't know," I said, calmly taking the fork the rest of the way to my mouth in order to keep it busy chewing on food—instead of her ass! Was she serious? Not once did she apologize for hurting me so deeply.

Looking back, I realize my feelings towards this person tainted the thrill of this significant moment in my life. Not her fault. I let someone else steal my joy. Not until I hobbled into the banquet room the next afternoon wearing two different size shoes did the honor of winning the prestigious award hit me.

We sat at a table with reporters from the *Indiana Gazette*. I think the food tasted good, I don't remember what was served or eating before the presentations.

As each person walked up to the small stage in the front of the room, I watched as he or she shook hands with the presenter, accepted the award, acknowledged applause, and then returned to his or her seat. I had the routine down pat but worried about the bigger shoe falling off my tender, swollen foot as I stepped on and off the stage. Fear vanished as soon as I heard my name.

I held my head high and walked toward the stage to receive the state's highest award for investigative reporting. The presenter handed me a wooden plaque in the shape of a keystone with my name engraved on a metal plate attached to the front, and then shook my hand. As I turned to step off the stage, watching my feet all the way, I heard many hands clapping along with a few whistles coming from a table in front of the stage on the right.

I looked up and saw a white sign sticking up in the center of the round table with *Pittsburgh Press* printed in black letters on top and *Pittsburgh Post Gazette* directly beneath. Reporters from the two of the largest newspapers in Pittsburgh cheered me on which made me float back to my seat on cloud nine.

"You are the only reason I'm here," my fellow reporter said, staring at the award she now held in her hands. "This award is for investigative reporting. You did the investigation. I came in after it was pretty much over."

I knew how much the award meant to her. She told me she dreamt of winning it the night we celebrated. Looking back, I wish

I could have told her how happy I was to share the honor with her, which would have made the moment so much sweeter—instead of resenting her presence at the table.

Driving home after the ceremony with the state's highest award for journalism on the seat next to me felt strange, good and sad at the same time. I guess I expected people to share my pride and happiness—those darn rose-colored glasses again! Truth is, my green-eyed coworkers stabbed me in the back way before the award was announced. Funny how people want to knock you down, keep you small. Let me just say, never, ever give in or listen to anyone who does not support your dreams and success—even your own parents.

My mother came to my apartment to acknowledge my achievement. Her comment wasn't very funny then but good for a laugh now. "I know exactly what I'm going to get you for winning the award," she said, walking out of the bathroom towards me in the living room, with an impish smile on her face. "A new toilet seat. That cracked, padded thing you got in there pinches my ass."

Funny, I was tired of being pinched, too. Two months after receiving the award, I sadly placed my press pass, key to the front door, and resignation letter in an envelope and dropped it in the OUT box at the office. Then packed up my few personal belongings and walked out the door.

# TWENTY-TWO

*Whenever a separation is made between liberty and justice, neither, in my opinion, is safe.*

EDMUND BURKE

Things quieted down following the second autopsy. I did freelance work for the *Pittsburgh Post Gazette* and worked as a temporary information consultant for Westinghouse as the family continued searching for the truth.

When John told the press he'd drive to the state attorney general's door to get someone to investigate this case, the then Attorney General Ernie Preate, Jr. told reporters he'd investigate if the family made the request. Elaine immediately sent a letter asking him to investigate her son's death. She also sent letters to U.S. Senator John Heinz and Pennsylvania State Senator Frank Pecora of Penn Hills. Elaine knew Senator Heinz personally from working with Fred Rogers.

Senator Heinz contacted the state attorney general, who responded by saying he had faith in the investigation now being handled by the Indiana County district attorney; and the state attorney general had no power whatsoever to intervene.

"The untimely death of individuals such as this are always very heart-rending," Preate wrote Senator Heinz. "This case, of course, was not helped any by the conflict of opinions rendered by the two pathologists who performed autopsies. However, the trauma to the head found in the second autopsy is not inconsistent with an alcohol-related accidental death. I know that the parents of these types of decedents are rarely satisfied that their loved ones were not killed by some outside force."

Didn't anybody get it? No alcohol detected in his blood at the time of death! Made you want to scream! All the family had to do was make the request, so he could deny it? Frustrating, very frustrating. Around and around they went, no end in sight. I should have counted how many times public officials and others who examined this case continued to insist he was drunk and that's why he died—even with three skull fractures and a brain hemorrhage staring them in the face!

There was NO alcohol! NO vomit! Microscopic slides of lung tissue, the toxicology report and second autopsy proved it! Could or would anyone ever get that through their thick heads?

As soon as the district attorney reopened the investigation, my hands were tied. I couldn't call anyone or be involved with the case without being charged with obstruction of justice. I had to let go. John, Elaine and I spoke occasionally to see if anyone heard anything about the ongoing investigation.

"That's the way it goes," I told John one night. "You have to climb up the ladder one step at a time. First the Indiana County district attorney; next the state attorney general, then the F.B.I and the United States Department of Justice."

During the first few months, John called the D.A. to ask about the case. By the end of March 1991, the family grew restless. Elaine sent a new letter to the Indiana County D.A. outlining the family's concerns and questions.

"Many people have asked why we are so insistent in bringing up his death after so long," she wrote. "Our question is: what would you do if it were your son? As we have said all along, all we want is the truth. We are asking you, as the District Attorney of Indiana County, not to close this case until this truth is found by whatever means. If foul play cannot be ruled out, but your office cannot obtain evidence or statements to verify some type of conclusion, we—the family of Jack Davis—request the action of a grand jury be carefully considered."

An article published in the *Indiana Gazette* prompted the district attorney to request a meeting with John in his office. John accused the Indiana County D.A. with "dragging its feet" and discussed the letters sent to U.S. Senator Heinz, Pennsylvania Senator Pecora, and the state attorney general.

"When it's over, if the FBI or attorney general wants to come in and look at our findings, that's fine with me," the D.A. told reporters.

John and Marisa showed up in the D.A.'s office, tape recorder and questions in hand. The district attorney, along with members of his task force and Coroner Streams, greeted them. He wanted John to explain the cover-up he kept talking about in the press. Streams told John, Wecht said Jack fell and that is what they are going on.

That said, the meeting turned into one argument after another; the D.A. said he was doing everything he was supposed to be doing in this investigation. John read a list of the things he wasn't doing and the family wanted done now. He also let it slip that the IUP officer had read his police report to him and was the only person in Indiana that wanted to help his family.

Coincidentally, the officer was fired from the university a few weeks later. John shot his mouth in the wrong place at the wrong time. Marisa told me later, the new task force was made up of the same officers on the case when Jack died, except for the IUP officer.

"Why would they want to prove themselves wrong the first time?" she said on the phone that night.

Trust did not come easy at this time. The Indiana County district attorney quietly closed the investigation exactly one year later, November 1991. No one contacted the family. I happened to find out while doing research for a local magazine.

The editor, who was eager to publish a story about the case, encouraged my progress daily. I focused on tying up loose ends and finally got in touch with the former IUP Public Safety Director in Virginia. He left the university in February 1988 for personal reasons but officially resigned in April. He recalled being in the stairwell the night Jack's body was found.

"I'm sympathetic with the family, but I don't think they will ever find out what happened to him," he said.

As soon as I brought up the toxicology report and Dr. Griffin's explanation about alcohol metabolizing out of his blood after death, the former director said he had to go and hung up. I called back the next day.

"I just have one more question, did you notice blood on Jack's face?"

"I remember there was a lot of blood and I remember talking about it during the autopsy. I didn't know if it came from his mouth or his nose. No one ever explained why all that blood was there. I remember there were no bruises on the body except a cut over his left eye; that's why we didn't believe he was beaten or fell down."

I was surprised he remembered so many details years later.

"The university didn't do anything wrong as far as the investigation goes," he said. "I wouldn't do anything different."

"Do you remember discussing the results of the toxicology report with your investigating officer?"

"We talked about many things. It's possible that we discussed it."

"What did you think when the report came back with no alcohol detected in the blood?" I said, feeling comfortable enough to ask the loaded question at that point—but he abruptly ended the conversation.

The next day, I took a chance and contacted the now former IUP officer who investigated this case at his home, figuring since he didn't work for the university any more he might be willing to open up more. His attitude surprised me right off the bat.

"I have severed all ties in every way, shape, or form with the university and the state. I'm no longer a police officer and don't have to answer to the university or the state," he said "All I know is that poor Jack Davis ended up dead in the stairwell."

When I began to ask a specific question, he interrupted.

"How's this? I'll tell you the truth in the year 2010," he said. "Give me a call then." Click.

His comment bothered me for years. Why 2010? Was he being sarcastic?

The next day, I tried to set up another interview with Dr. Griffin. "I'm not interested in discussing this," he said.

"I'm writing a magazine story about the case and would like to include your side of the story," I said.

"I'm not interested in making this public," he replied.

"I just want the article to be fair," I said.

There was no response and he didn't hang up.

"The toxicology report says," and that's as far as I got.

At this point, I decided to make an appointment to interview the university's vice president. The IUP public relations director scheduled the meeting and the IUP public safety director would attend. When the editor heard, he suggested going with me.

"It might help if you are with someone who wears a suit and tie," he said. "I don't mean to offend you with that comment."

That was the first time during this entire investigation anyone ever equated my gender with disadvantage. The thought had never crossed my mind until that moment. At first, his words stung but as we traveled up, down and around those very familiar country roads on our way to Indiana, I felt relieved not to have to go it alone.

Finding out security guards checked the doors of the science building between two and four on the mornings of October 16 through October 20 turned out to be the only new information gathered that day.

"They probably parked in the rear of the building near the loading dock and walked around," The IUP public safety director said. "They probably only checked the main outside doors in the front and back."

We also discussed Jack's fraternity and the toxicology report during the taped interview. IUP Vice President Edward Receski said they had nothing to do with the off-campus group that lost its national charter and university recognition. As for the toxicology report, he referred me to Coroner Streams.

"I think you better understand that the county coroner makes those decisions. Indiana University of Pennsylvania doesn't make those decisions. Indiana University of Pennsylvania does not perform an autopsy, Indiana University of Pennsylvania does not make statements as to toxicology reports, drug reports, etc. and so forth. That's not our line of work. The county coroner is the man in charge."

"Wouldn't somebody have questioned the fact that the report came back with no alcohol found in his body?" I said.

"I think there were a lot of questions asked and a lot of explanations given. I think at the time when the explanations were given as to the fact to what was involved and the explanation of the coroner, the professional person, we didn't second-guess a professional person. We are not professionals, we are far away from it," the university vice president said. "If you can find the solution to this thing we would be very grateful."

# TWENTY-THREE

*Justice in the life and conduct of the State is possible only as it first resides in the hearts and souls of the citizens.*

AUTHOR UNKNOWN

To round out the magazine article, I met with Jack's mother again—this time alone in her apartment on Sunday afternoon. Jack's very familiar high school senior portrait used in every newspaper and newscast caught my eye as soon as I walked into her living room. She had the original eight-by-ten color version.

"He was my only natural born child," she said. "I had a lot of hopes and dreams for him just like other parents have for their children."

Jack was three years old when she married John Lynch, Sr.

"I was an only child," she said. "Jack moved in with his brothers and sisters. They treated him like he was their own baby brother right away. He fit right in with his two new younger sisters."

She explained she always had trouble expressing anger about anything. "I'm just not that kind of person. I got very depressed when Jack died. I had to go to counseling for a long time. I didn't think I would ever be able to live a normal life again. Of course, nothing will ever be the same."

She talked about the night they found her son's body and how she could only deal with that at the time, "You think it is a bad dream and you'll wake up soon but you never do."

Although we had talked often on the phone, I saw a different side of her that day. She appeared calm and collected, thinking over every word before she spoke. When the investigation began, I often wondered why she wasn't outraged and demanding answers following her son's death.

I judged her, believing if that were my son, I'd raise holy hell and never rest until I found the truth. Well, that day I learned a big lesson. I have no idea how I'd react if my entire world shattered into tiny pieces in a matter of minutes, and pray never to find out.

"It's like having open heart surgery every day of your life without an anesthetic," she said. "You never forget. You just try to figure out how to keep living."

She said her son's death changed her forever. "I used to trust people. When the officials in Indiana told me what happened to Jack, I believed them. I trusted them to tell me the truth and could not imagine why they wouldn't tell me the truth. Now, I've learned not to trust anyone. That's very sad. That was the big lesson."

Realizing someone stole Jack's future also proved hard for her to accept. "He will never get married or have children. He was so young and had so much life to live," she said, pausing. "They took away part of my future, too."

At this point, it all seemed so senseless, no reason for her pain and suffering or why someone took her child's life. It made me wonder why one human being thinks they have the right to end the life and dreams of another for any reason whatsoever.

"I still hold a hope deep in my heart that one day someone will walk up to me and say, 'I know what happened to your son.' The hope will always be there."

For her sake, I hope so, too. If only life were that simple. Then again, who knows what the future may bring. Maybe, just maybe, someday someone somewhere will feel the need to unburden his or her conscience and find the courage to do the right thing and tell the truth. Even after the year 2010 has come and gone.

Talking to Elaine that day put a bee in my bonnet. Why not make posters with Jack's picture on them asking for information, then hang them everywhere and see what happens. John and Marisa agreed to create them and use their phone number for the hotline. Five years almost to the day his body was found, John plastered posters around campus and on telephone poles all over Indiana. He also hung them on telephone poles around Penn Hills, thinking maybe Jack's former classmates might know something.

The next day, the *Indiana Gazette* ran a story; the reporter called the hotline and assured readers their comments would be kept strictly confidential. The new Indiana County district attorney who took over when D.A. Martin won his bid for judge was not pleased.

"If anyone has any information they should call the Indiana Borough police," Handler said in the article. "If there is any legitimate information, we'll follow up on it through appropriate jurisdiction. We will determine if further investigation is warranted."

Several hotline calls turned out to be dead ends. However, a message from one former IUP student proved quite interesting. She said she didn't come forward earlier because the accused bartender lived next door to her and she didn't want to be involved.

She said she saw Jack at the bar that night with his fraternity brothers, whom she knew well. They were making a big deal out of Jack partying with them because he seldom did. Jack left the bar around midnight.

"He was happy sitting at the bar. He didn't get thrown out while I was there," she said. "Jack's big brother was a trouble maker and I know first hand he gave Jack cocaine. I attended their fraternity parties on a pretty regular basis."

As a matter of fact, she left the bar and headed to a party at the fraternity house that night and claims Jack was there when she arrived.

"I remember distinctly that Jack was there because his frat brothers were still joking with him because he was at the party," the girl said. "He didn't usually attend."

She placed Jack in the fraternity house around 12:30 or 1:00 a.m., the same time Tom Brennan said he walked Jack back to campus. Definitely interesting and it gets even more interesting. She also witnessed the fight between Jack's fraternity and the Phi Delts next door.

"All the frat brothers went outside, including Jack," she said. "But I never saw Jack come back in."

This was the same fight described in the paper as a "shouting match" police had to break up. She said when Jack was missing she went to the police to tell them where and when she last saw him alive. There was no record in either police report.

"The police actually drove me around in a police car behind the fraternity house looking for Jack's body near the railroad tracks," she said. "I was right there in the car! I even remember

215

thinking what if they did find his body! I was scared, very scared." I listened amazed, to put it mildly.

"If the family wants me to be hypnotized, if that will help them, I'll do it," she said with conviction. "Maybe I can remember more about that night and then they'll know I am telling the truth."

If she was telling the truth that meant someone else was not. Then again, maybe the other kid did walk Jack back to campus, the time being the mistake. Did Jack leave him and go to the fraternity party and then what happened for five days? How did he end up back on campus in the stairwell close to where the kid supposedly left him that night? Was his body placed there on purpose? He could have been thrown in the lake or buried in the woods that surround the small country town—never to be found.

Another caller told John she heard Jack was arrested and beaten in a jail cell. Did he have a fake I.D. that night to get into the bar? He supposedly encountered police twice during fights that night. My thoughts ran in so many directions looking at any and all possibilities.

All I knew is Jack had to be alive somewhere for five days, a place where he could eat, pull down his pants to move his bowels and wipe himself clean, unzip his pants to urinate, but not shave. Also, based on the stages of rigor mortis, he could not have been dead for more than twenty-four hours when found.

You may recall, Jack's brother Mike said, when he went down into the stairwell and touched Jack's chest, it was hard. During the process of rigor mortis the muscles gradually contract and the body stiffens within the first twelve hours of death, and then it takes another twelve hours for the muscles to completely relax and the body goes limp.

Someone also sent John a clipping from a small suburban paper called the *North Hills News Record* dated July 18, 1991. The headline read, *"Crime at College—Student Guide to Safety."*

In the article, Indiana University of Pennsylvania is listed as one of the safest universities in the country with the lowest crime rate in the northeast United States. The statistic was compiled by Federal Bureau of Investigation and also brought another one to mind.

"Do you know that Indiana County has the highest suicide rate per capita in the country," my fellow reporter said one day on the phone. We joked about the kid Coroner Streams based his ruling on in this case working overtime since the coroner's entire theory about Jack's death depended on this one student's statement. Her comment, however, made us both wonder about other deaths in Indiana.

I'm pretty sure every county in this country does not have a forensic pathologist running for or elected county coroner. Makes you wonder why these extremely important positions are filled via political elections instead of governments hiring the most qualified person to do the job based on medical qualifications and scientific expertise. Mr. Streams, an ambulance driver, had to depend on a hospital pathologist to assist him with his coroner duties. A medical doctor who may or may not know a body ceases to function after death.

Add to the mix a state university, like most colleges and universities that are constantly trying to protect, maintain, and project an image of a safe environment in order to attract students and maintain enrollment. Not only is state funding based on enrollment numbers, the economic survival of the town or city in which the institute of high learning is located depends on the health and wealth of the hand that feeds them.

The *Indiana Gazette* ran an article on January 18, 1990 with the headline, "*IUP economic impact on county at $155 million.*" The figures were based on an economic impact study conducted by a Pittsburgh consulting firm hired by IUP and outlines "impressive economic and social effects of the university on the community."

The study revealed that IUP brings in over $155 million and some 5,465 jobs into Indiana County annually. Plus, the over 13,000 students on the main campus spent $34.5 million in local business establishments with faculty and staff contributing another $16.9 million.

> "A significant portion of the county's employment is indirectly the result of IUP," the study says. "Through the purchase of goods and services, IUP and its faculty, staff and students generate non-university employment in the county, which in turn generates other jobs."

Just some interesting info we picked up along the way.

# TWENTY-FOUR

*It's no wonder that truth is stranger than fiction.
Fiction has to make sense.*

MARK TWAIN

We learned many things during the first two years of the investigation. The family now knew Jack did not walk down into the stairwell intoxicated to urinate, pass out and choke to death on his own vomit. The second autopsy proved three skull fractures and a major brain hemorrhage caused his death.

Even though the press moved on to the next big story, the family's desperate search for the truth continued taking them in different directions. For instance, one day I ended up talking with a psychic over the phone. I have no clue how we connected back then.

This jaw-dropping experience started with a woman known as "Idaho Elk," who said she worked on the Atlanta child murders, a case that dominated the national news for months several years ago, and could help with this case.

"Let's see what she has to say," I said to Marisa. "What harm can it do?"

We scheduled a three-way conference call one evening, Marisa and I both in our own homes on separate lines and the psychic in, you guessed it, Idaho. Beforehand, we agreed if either one of us felt uncomfortable for any reason and at any time, we'd hang up and let the other person finish the call.

"Do you want to know what the murderer was thinking first or the victim?" the woman said from almost a thousand miles away.

The question freaked me out. I didn't want to hear what the murderer thought while beating Jack to death or Jack's last thoughts as his life ended. We discussed both disgusting options and went with Jack.

"Intoxication is the focus of this case," Idaho Elk said, immediately blowing me away. Marisa gasped. She knew nothing, absolutely nothing, about this case—no names, no details.

"He is being taken to this big fancy house surrounded by water; they store a lot of cocaine there," the psychic said. "He was beaten on a dirt road then dragged to this house. He was locked in some kind of small room, like a closet. It was dark."

She paused. "I see three pairs of shoes," she said, pausing again. "There's a light coming through a space under the door." She described the shoes then her eyes traveled up each pair of legs, their bodies then faces. "There are three men. One is a police officer with bright red hair, almost orange..." Click. Marisa hung up.

"One guy looks like someone you would see in a mafia movie. Tough," she continued without pause. "The other is a young man, perhaps a student of some kind."

I stretched out on my couch, totally numb from head to toe. My hand clutched the receiver of the phone so tight my fingers cramped, my ear hurt. Every fiber in my body screamed, "No more! Hang up!" I couldn't.

"He was involved with these people and they were involved in selling drugs," she said. "He knew he was going to be hurt because he knew their secrets. They kept him at the house and gave him drugs to keep him alive."

The story sounded so real, so believable, as if she really did see through Jack's eyes. True or not, one-by-one large, warm, salty tears rolled sideways off my face, splashing onto the hand holding the phone against my now very wet ear.

"He remembers being carried down into a stairwell and says that is when the whitewash began," she said, stopping abruptly.

"Did you say, stairwell?" I said, making sure I heard right before freaking out.

"Yes," she replied, "Five guys carried him down the steps and left him there."

How in the world did she know about the stairwell!

"I can't listen any more!" I said, dazed.

"Don't you want to hear what the murderer was thinking?" she said, apparently not hearing the trembling in my voice.

"I can't," I said, insides shivering. "Thank you for your time."

Marisa picked up on the first ring.

"Boy, that was really something," I said. "What made you hang up so fast?"

"When she described the police officer with the bright orange, red hair, I couldn't listen anymore," she said. Her voice sounded as if she had just seen a ghost. "The IUP police officer on the district attorney's task force had bright red-orange hair. All I could see was his face. He was there when we met with the D.A. It just struck too close to home."

"Well, wait until you hear the rest," I said, listening to her gasp—especially when I got to the part about the stairwell.

The eerie experience haunted me for weeks. I told everyone about the psychic from Idaho, even my hairdresser, Steve. We'd known each other for years. He always asked about the case as he snipped split ends and touched up roots.

"You need to lighten up," he said, smiling as he slid a comb through my long, dark brown hair.

"You can say that again!" I replied, not realizing he meant my hair.

He talked me into adding a few blonde highlights that day and every visit thereafter until my whole head turned reddish blonde, which lasted about a year. He listened quietly as his hands painted individual strands of my hair with thick, white paste, then quickly wrapped each one in aluminum foil and patted them down into layers all around my head with the pointy end of the brush. He nodded occasionally as I told the tale of Idaho Elk, complete with startled facial expressions to emphasize scary parts. He only interrupted when I mentioned the big house on the lake.

"Sounds like the house I stayed at for a weekend up there with some friends," he said, wide-eyed and amazed by the possible connection. "I knew some kids who went to IUP and we used to party together in Indiana on the weekends. It was like a big estate on the lake. We went boating up there on that lake; it was a lot of fun. There was a big party that weekend and I still remember the big bowls of cocaine they were passing around and offering everyone."

Did he just pour ice water on my head? Chills shivered my spine. His words gave the psychic's vision a foothold in the real world, perhaps just a little too much reality for a five-dollar tip. I drove home, imagining what Jack might have suffered before death. Right then and there, I vowed never to repeat the story again. Of course, you know what they say, "Never say never."

Since there was nothing new going on in the investigation, the family and I contacted each other sporadically over the next two years. One day, Marisa called out of the blue to say Elaine was going to speak with a psychic from Ohio someone recommended and wanted me to go with her. Just the thought of listening to another psychic turned my stomach and set my teeth on edge. Elaine didn't know about Idaho Elk.

We met with the psychic in a local motel on a Saturday morning; he was in town for the weekend. I walked through the door defiant, sarcastic words dipped in disdain on the tip of my tongue. My arms folded tightly across my chest, perhaps to protect myself from any more pain.

Elaine and the psychic sat opposite each other at the small round, motel room table next to the curtained window. As instructed, I pulled a chair up to the side of the table and squeezed in between the bed on my left and Elaine on my right. "I want to talk to my son," she said calmly with absolute conviction.

I squirmed, desperate to escape the sound of their voices. It was no use; my heart ached as she spoke to her dead child. I cry typing these words. I cannot repeat their conversation; it is not mine to share. At one point, I looked over at Elaine's face and understood completely, she never had the chance to say good-bye.

After a while, the man sitting there, eyes shut, supposedly channeling Jack, disgusted me, turning my pain into anger.

"He's putting on one hell of a show!" I thought shaking my head, "Charlatan!"

I had to look away, study the walls, the corny pictures you always find in motel rooms, the floor, anything to avoid making a spectacle out of myself. My eyes scanned the room looking for anything to distract my attention: two double beds, flowered bedspreads, no personal items anywhere, television, remote, and then my brain screamed!

"Did he just say big house on a lake!"

I stared as if blasted by a stun gun listening to the psychic describe being taken into this big house—he even described the tiles on the floor—where he was beaten, then put in this small, dark room like a closet or something!

"Oh, my God!" I kept saying to myself as I squirmed in my seat unable to believe my own ears.

"He sees a slice of light coming though a crack under door," the psychic said. I wanted to run away but instead gasped loudly several times.

"There are three pairs of shoes," he said, eyes still shut, speaking as Jack.

I can't for the life of me remember what he said about the shoes. I know he mentioned not being able to see very far up their legs. At that point, my brain shut down, numbing my senses. This was too much! He said almost the exact same words and painted the same exact picture as Idaho Elk two years before! How was that possible?

I looked at Elaine, an astonished look on my face, my head moving side to side. She glanced over for a second with a quizzical look on her face then quickly turned back, intent on hearing every word. I stared down at my hands now neatly folded in my lap until, thankfully, our one-hour session ended.

At lunch, I told her about Idaho Elk. Now we both looked totally freaked out sitting in the restaurant silently eating our sandwiches. You can probably guess what we both thought at that moment, "Since both psychics said pretty much the exact same thing, could the story be true?"

Again, Jack had to be somewhere alive, eating and using a bathroom from Friday until at least twenty-four hours before his body was found. Maybe Indiana Borough Detective Sergeant Antolik was right from the start. Jack was abducted.

Perhaps one might view talking to psychics as the act of a desperate person and that would be right in this instance. The family had nowhere else to turn. The Indiana County district attorney closed the investigation exactly one year later; no new leads, another dead end.

Then one summer night, in June 1993, while lying on the couch watching television and switching channels during commercials with the remote, I came across a show called *Unsolved Mysteries*. I'd heard of the program before but never paid much attention.

"Hmm," I thought, "Maybe they'd be interested."

The letter went out a few days later along with the hope that maybe, just maybe, they'd televise the story and somewhere someone watching would pick up the phone ready to clear their guilty conscience—and spill his or her guts! There was nothing to lose.

Much to my surprise—I mean I was really, really surprised—a producer from *Unsolved Mysteries* called my house about a year later, ready to go! Turns out, when Dr. Wecht published a book with a chapter dedicated to this case, someone remembered the letter tucked away in a file somewhere. Goes to show you, you just never know.

The production company rolled into town sometime in June 1994 to film a segment focused on world-renowned forensic pathologist, Dr. Cyril Wecht at work on one of his most interesting cases.

I provided background information but politely refused to appear on camera. Being in any kind of spotlight did not appeal to me at the time. I preferred watching from the sidelines.

"You're a key figure in this case," the producer said. "If you're concerned about your personal safety, being on television provides you with greater safety."

I finally agreed, not because of all the cajoling or pressure but because away from the noisy hubbub that surrounded our exciting new venture my heart quietly whispered, "It's the right thing to do."

# TWENTY-FIVE

*What we have in us of the image of God
is the love of truth and justice.*

Demosthenes

We were tickled pink! I even made a trip to the mall (shopping is not my forte) to buy a new outfit for the show. Not that I could afford it—but this was a nationally televised program with millions of viewers. No slapping on my usual ragged cut-off blue jean shorts and Steelers T-shirt. I spent hours going from store to store and finally found the perfect outfit. A semi-dressy black pantsuit with a delicate, white design stitched on front, elegant yet professional with a little sass thrown in for good measure.

Of course, we all hoped to meet the narrator of the program, 1940's film star legend, Robert Stack, and felt slightly let down when told he filmed his part in Hollywood. No matter. Just being a part of the process turned out to be exciting and interesting. Production took almost three weeks. No, we didn't get paid. Of course, I can't speak for Dr. Wecht, the star of the show.

The film crew crammed lights, cameras and props all around the living room in an enormous house rented to shoot interviews with the family. Let me just say, sitting under hot, bright lights for what feels like forever as someone asks a multitude of questions is not only unnerving but a lesson unto itself. I now know I'd crack in less than an hour under police interrogation.

"What do you think happened to Jack?" proved to be the hardest question to answer.

I spoke slowly, choosing words carefully, not wanting to ramble on like a babbling idiot or point the finger at anyone on national television.

Instead, I blurted out every theory that crossed my mind during the investigation, including Jack being abducted, arrested, injured in a fight between fraternities and hunted down and beaten to death.

Elaine, Jack Sr. and John were interviewed sitting together on a long, blue couch in the living room. I sat on the steps in the hallway listening as they discussed disputed facts and their ongoing search for the truth. Reenacting their first meeting with Dr. Wecht in the conference room at his office is the only time we all appeared on camera together.

My job was to reach across the table and hand the doctor a copy of the toxicology report; their job was to look interested. Other than Jack Sr.'s one line, Robert Stack narrated the scene, sounding like one of those hard-nosed private eyes you see in classic black and white detective movies. The deep tone of his voice could turn a diaper commercial complete with smiling babies happily crawling around on the floor, into a dangerous, sinister drama.

Once, as they say, "the film was in the can," the production company moved on and our wait began. We had no idea how they pieced together the story, which was scheduled to air in November but was delayed until January 6, 1995. When the big day finally arrived, my family crammed into my now tinier living room to watch the premier with me. I had to move into a smaller place with lower rent for financial reasons.

We toasted the occasion with a few sips of Bailey's Irish Cream over ice as soon as we heard Robert Stack's dramatic voice open the show with a brief synopsis and glimpse of the three stories featured that Friday night.

"*In law enforcement circles Dr. Cyril Wecht has become a legend. One case continues to haunt him, the mysterious death of a 20-year-old college student near Pittsburgh, Pennsylvania. Perhaps tonight you can provide the clue that helps Dr. Wecht solve this controversial mystery.*"

He mentioned two more segments but I couldn't tell you what they were about if my live depended on it. I sat on pins and needles through at least ten commercials, anxious to see the long-awaited finished product.

"*He has been called a real live Quincy, the modern day Sherlock Holmes, by any name Dr. Cyril Wecht is undeniably one of the country's top forensic pathologists. In court, it is Wecht's testimony that often tips the balance.*"

Other cases he solved were mentioned and then Dr. Wecht was shown reenacting the examination of a body, wearing green surgical scrubs. Then the camera moved down into the stairwell, where an actor lay at the bottom in the same contorted position as Jack did. I gasped. Reenactment of this part of the story had never crossed my mind. My stomach muscles tensed thinking his mother, father, brothers and sisters were sitting in front of their television sets at that very moment watching the nightmare come alive years later in living color.

The actor, bearing a slight resemblance to Jack and wearing his fraternity jacket, staggers drunk across campus on national television. He grabs the red railing sticking out of the top of the stairwell, looks around then walks down into the hole as Robert

Stack explains the Indiana County coroner's original scenario. The camera then switched to Dr. Wecht in his office disputing Streams.

*"That body could not have been thrown down and he could not have stumbled because there were no bruises, abrasions, or contusions. That didn't fit,"* Dr. Wecht said. *"It's more likely Jack died or was unconscious or dying somewhere else and placed in the stairwell."*

The show held a few surprises such as the interview with Indiana Borough Detective Sergeant Antolik.

*"Personally, despite what anyone says I go with the fact that he fell from up above. He could have hit the walls. I've seen very strange things with drunks. There's nothing I wouldn't believe."*

My part ran close to the end. They cut my over one-hour interview into three sentences. *"That night there were fights reported between rival fraternities, perhaps he was involved and injured and they didn't know what to do with him. Maybe they kept him somewhere hoping he would get better. When he didn't, they put him in the stairwell."*

Boy, was I naive! Being the investigator in the case, I expected all my theories to air but the one they choose to let come out of my mouth made his death sound so innocent.

I did, however, learn a couple new facts from the show. Approximately two hundred students used classrooms with windows overlooking the stairwell during the five days in question. Not one reported seeing the body. Also, according to Dr. Wecht, Jack had to be alive for at least thirty hours for alcohol to metabolize out of his body, based on the assumption he drank alcohol the night he disappeared.

The statistic of thirty hours to metabolize the alcohol out of his blood is an important aspect in this case for a couple reasons.

Based on the absence of alcohol in his blood at the time of death you can rule out Streams' theory that he died at 2 a.m. Saturday. More importantly, however, is according the original autopsy report, Jack died with five hundred cubic centimeters, a little more than one pint or sixteen ounces of partially digested food in his stomach, which means, if his body metabolized the alcohol out of his body within thirty hours, it would have also metabolized the food out of his stomach with the alcohol. And, since it takes at least, let's be generous, from five to eight hours to digest food, one can conclude Jack died shortly after eating a meal.

Based on the amount of stomach contents, no alcohol in his blood, and his body being in the twenty-four hour rigor mortis cycle when found at ten-twenty Wednesday night, I believe Jack's life ended sometime after dinner Tuesday night, as his parents scoured the small town searching for their only child.

Physical evidence, the weather in particular, also points to his body being moved into the stairwell sometime Wednesday. It poured Tuesday and his clothes were dry.

One can only guess what story his missing organs might have told concerning his whereabouts—if not misplaced somehow during the autopsy. Blood pools in specific places within each internal organ based on the position of the dead body. The scientific term is livor mortis or postmortem lividity.

To get a clearer picture, let's say a person is found dead lying on his stomach, the blood would pool in the organs towards the front of the body; in a sitting position at the bottom and of course, towards the back if the person is lying face up.

"Had he lived Jack Davis would have graduated with 2,700 other students in the class of 1989 at Indiana University of Pennsylvania. Cyril Wecht is convinced that among them is at least one person that *really knows what happened to Jack Alan Davis, Jr. Perhaps the time has finally come to set the record straight."*

Robert Stack narrated to the end. Jack's high school portrait appeared on screen above the eight hundred number to call with information. A few weeks later, a Federal Express envelope arrived with a small stack of computer printouts listing calls received. Most came from viewers looking for a way to contact Wecht about their own cases, some voiced opinions about Jack's case and others left messages related to Jack's death.

The Indiana County district attorney also received the same printouts, plus one viewer sent a letter directly to his office which came to me years later.

> *February 10, 1995*
>
> *District Attorney:*
>
> *I recently watched Unsolved Mysteries on television and saw the segment on the death of Jack Davis. I was a student at IUP during that time period and I might have some info regarding the case.*
>
> *My friend was a close friend of Jack and the Sigma Tau Fraternity. One night about 2 or 3 years after his death this person told me something. She said that Jack had died (of what, I'm not quite sure—drugs or rough housing?) In a house where some of the fraternity brothers had lived and they kept him in a closet (dead) for a couple of days because they were scared or just didn't know what to do.*
>
> *I never told anyone else this because the case had been closed and I wasn't even sure of who or what had happened.*

> I'm writing to you in lieu of telephoning because I really would not like to get involved but I wanted to help if I could."

No name or contact information included. Did the reference to Jack being put in a closet hit you, too? Another viewer that called the toll free number left this message:

"Caller is from Clarion, PA and she was a student at Indiana University of Pennsylvania in 1987. Caller claims that the fraternities are really closed mouthed in that community and finding information will be difficult. Caller believes that the Sigma boys were very violent and lost their charter and they were very capable of killing and hiding the body. Caller wishes to remain anonymous and will not give any names."

Again, no contact information left, which made reading the messages frustrating to say the least. There was no way to follow up possible leads, even when the information pointed to murder.

"Caller said that he won't give us his name. He said that Jack Davis did not die accidentally but he was killed at the university nearby where his body was found."

Each person that called the toll-free number was asked, "May we forward your name/phone# to the law enforcement working on this case?" The majority said no.

"Caller says that his fraternity may have done it but can't tell because of the fraternity code of silence."

The calling center received several crank calls, mostly information based on hearsay and rumors, and also from psychics hoping their visions might help solve the mystery.

"Caller says that Jack Davis Jr. was hit on the head by a long object that is rounded on one end. She said she knows for sure that he was murdered. I asked caller how she knows this information and she said that she SEES these things. She is psychic but does not call herself one. This is all the information she SAW."

A unique and interesting experience for sure, frustrating at best. Reading the messages left me feeling helpless with no way to separate fact from fiction.

"Caller says she dated someone who went to the school and this guy told her a story about this incident. Caller says the boy, who attended school at the campus from 1986-1991, told her that he was afraid to go to authorities. Caller says the guy told her that members of Davis's fraternity knew what had happened to him and that Jack had been killed, possibly during a fight. Caller says her ex-boyfriend told her that Jack was kept in a cooler in the basement after his death and then left at the bottom of the stairs. Caller says her ex-boyfriend was in a fraternity at the time, but not the same frat as Jack. Caller says there were many stories circulating around campus, but caller's ex-boyfriend says members of the fraternity community knew what happened to Jack. Caller says she will not give her ex-boyfriend's name or contact information because he is a very abusive person and she does not keep in touch with him at all. Caller wanted to pass along this information...and hopes members of Jack's fraternity can be questioned...caller thinks it was Jack's own fraternity that was somehow involved in his death."

The last call listed on the printout restated the hearsay rumor we'd heard immediately after the three-part series ran in the *Tribune-Review*.

"Caller says that someone told her that someone else vomited on the victim to make it look like the victim's own vomit. Caller heard about the story from someone who was in a fraternity at the same time the crime happened."

Unfortunately, using the nationally televised program to find answers produced even more gruesome questions. The experience itself, however, offered new insight. I now understood how exasperated law enforcement agencies must feel when no one is willing to come forward, go on record or bear witness and their criminal cases dead end.

Especially when you know in your heart of hearts someone somewhere absolutely positively knows exactly what happened. Of course, one can always hold on to the satisfaction of knowing that keeping a secret of this magnitude locked up inside yourself for the rest of your life will slowly devour your sanity.

# TWENTY-SIX

*I think the first duty of society is justice.*

ALEXANDER HAMILTON

Coming up empty handed after the show aired dealt the family a hard blow. I felt it, too. After all was said and done, the biggest unsolved mystery seemed to be how to get to the truth. Was Wecht right? Did the family miss their only opportunity to find answers when the two-year statute of limitations for filing civil lawsuits expired?

"Why can't they file suits with all this new evidence?" I wondered then headed to a local law library to research statues. "There has to be some way to get this into court."

Turns out, they had another option. I called John and Elaine to explain that as private citizens they had the right to file their own criminal complaints with the Indiana County district attorney. Perhaps the chances of getting their case heard in court were slim to none but you never know unless you try. They agreed.

I spent the next three days following examples out of borrowed law books to draw up two formal criminal complaints. Exactly ten days after watching *Unsolved Mysteries,* John drove the three of us to Indiana; we spent the night in a motel. Early the next morning, we walked in the Indiana County district attorney's office and Elaine filed charges against Coroner Streams and Dr. Griffin.

We sat opposite the investigator across a large, brown, wooden desk presenting evidence for hours. Afterwards, he explained the D.A. would consider the facts then decide whether their case held merit.

Elaine and John charged Streams with criminal conspiracy, obstructing justice, hindering the apprehension or prosecution of a criminal, and abuse of office. They charged Dr Griffin with criminal conspiracy, providing false reports to law enforcement, tampering with or fabricating evidence, tampering with public records, obstructing justice, and hindering the apprehension or prosecution of a criminal.

"Streams declined comment on the complaint yesterday, Griffin could not be reached for comment," said the article printed on the front page of the *Tribune-Review* the very next day, January 14, 1995.

> ...The Lynches say Streams and Griffin continued to perpetrate the alcohol/vomit theory even after toxicology reports showed there were only trace amounts of alcohol in Davis' stomach and urine.
>
> They say they are convinced Davis was murdered and his body carried down into the stairwell hours before the body was found.
>
> "Jack's body could not have been in that stairwell for five days because rain poured down in Indiana Tuesday and when his body was found Wednesday, his clothes were completely dry," said Mrs. Lynch. "Where was he?
>
> "I'd like to get these men in a courtroom under oath and get some answers. There are just too many things about this case that don't add up..."

Local television stations picked up the story immediately and headed straight to Elaine for comments. Coverage lasted one day—a flash in the pan, which didn't matter at this point. The goal now was to get the case into court.

It had been four years since the three-part series hit the front page of the *Tribune-Review*. I worked as a freelance journalist for years and finally decided it was not exactly my cup of tea. Perhaps this case left a bitter taste in my mouth about journalism in general or maybe walking into situations always looking for negative angles in order to create copy wore on me.

Within a week, I had a new job as a private investigator. I didn't have my own P.I. license but in Pennsylvania you can conduct investigations working under someone who is licensed. No more worrying about objectivity or feeling guilty about being involved with this case.

When I contacted the Indiana County D.A.'s office a month later to find out the status of the criminal charges, the investigator advised the family hire an attorney to present the complaints should the case go to court. Elaine immediately contacted one who took the case.

I had mixed feelings about him at first because of a comment he made in jest as we explained details.

"Sounds like a case of Barney Fife-ism," he said, looking at us, smiling.

No one laughed but our eyebrows definitely shot up.

In case the name doesn't ring a bell, Barney Fife was the character on a 1960's sitcom, *The Andy Griffith Show*. Andy Griffith played the sheriff in the small fictitious town of Mayberry. Actor Don Knotts played his comedic, bumbling sidekick. Barney Fife was so incompetent and scatterbrained he was only allowed to keep one bullet in the pocket of his uniform shirt to use in case of emergency.

I'm sure the attorney meant to lighten things up with his comment, but after all we'd been through, his words hit a raw nerve. "The difference is Barney Fife didn't lie," I said, wiping the smirk off his face. Talk about getting off on the wrong foot! Still, I felt relief. Now, they had an attorney to represent and advise them. A load was lifted—at least, that's what I thought—again.

We ended up meeting on a regular basis to discuss facts and strategy. Every document, video and audio tapes, newspaper clippings, interview transcripts—everything was copied for him. I also handed over a list of every person contacted including phone numbers and results. Now all he had to do was figure out what to do with it all.

He started out discussing the criminal complaints and exchanging information with the new Indiana County district attorney. Stepping into this case this late in the game had to be mind boggling for both of them.

"It's simple," I said a few weeks after he took over. "Take it down to the basics. Tell the district attorney the family wants to meet with Coroner Streams and Dr. Griffin in his office. Present them with their own documents and ask them to explain their findings. They can't do it! They can't because their own findings do not support their conclusion."

I asked him to find the toxicology report and autopsy addendum among the papers in front of him on his desk.

"See right here," I said, pointing at the toxicology report. "No alcohol detected in his blood at the time of death. Now, look at the autopsy addendum signed by Dr. Griffin. Even after the toxicology report proves there's no alcohol, he concludes Jack's death is alcohol-related."

His face lit up as if a light bulb went on in his head. He now understood the ace up his sleeve, and from that moment on, started turning the screws. So tight, the new D.A. asked if the family might consider dropping the charges.

"Are you kidding?" were the first words out of my mouth when Elaine called to discuss the latest development. "Why would you even consider dropping the charges?"

"I am not going to drop them," Elaine said, sounding as confused as I felt.

"Then don't worry about it. Just say you're not willing to drop the charges," I muttered, half listening while still pondering the situation. "Wait a minute. I know. Tell them you'll drop the charges if the D.A. asks the state attorney general to investigate Jack's death! What do you have to lose?"

After we hung up, I remembered the conversation John and I had years ago about climbing up the ladder of justice one rung at a time. Could this be the boost they needed?

Although the Indiana County district attorney verbally agreed to send a formal request to the state attorney general, he resigned before keeping his promise. Their attorney called us into his office to discuss the situation; we expected the worst. Elaine and I somberly walked into his office a few days later braced for bad news but instead looked at each other, puzzled, when we saw the sheepish little grin on his face.

"The case will be turned over to the state," he said, sitting back smugly in his chair, arms folded across his chest, looking pretty pleased with himself.

"What do you mean?" I said, now sadly wary of good news.

"The new district attorney has agreed to turn the investigation over to the state!" he said, with enough enthusiasm to turn our frowns upside down.

We left his office walking on air, elated, hopeful, and pleased. We talked about the possibility of a real live investigation all the way home and over the next several weeks. All of a sudden, a dim light flickered at the end of the very long, dark tunnel. Victory was at hand but no one held the brass ring just yet.

Three months later, we were headed back to the attorney's office. As soon as we took our seats on the side of his now very familiar desk, he leaned back in his chair, this time with a great big Cheshire cat smile plastered across his face.

"He sent the letter," he said, grinning from ear to ear. "The district attorney sent the letter requesting the state investigate this case."

We both stared, not sure how to react.

"I have a copy of the letter right here," he said, seeing disbelief on our faces.

I scanned the document and checked the signature. It was real. I glanced up, apparently with this gigantic question mark over my head because he read my mind.

"How did this happen?" he said with a little snicker. "I wrote it myself and sent it to him for his signature."

Turns out, the new Indiana County D.A. kept promising to write the letter and the attorney kept bugging him for a copy. Finally, the D.A. said he didn't have time to do it, so he offered his services.

"I wrote the letter," he said again, still smiling. "I sent it and he signed it."

"That's fantastic!" I said, overjoyed. "We made it!"

As agreed, Elaine dropped the criminal complaints the next day. The case would be turned over to the state attorney general for investigation. Nothing left to do but sit back and wait to see what happened next.

# TWENTY-SEVEN

*Justice, sir, is the great interest of man on earth.
It is the ligament which holds civilized beings
and civilized nations together.*

Daniel Webster

I received a copy of the letter sent to the state attorney general in the mail a few days later, ripped open the envelope with the strength of a ravenous beast, plopped down on the couch and read the words over and over again.

> "...We do not have the resources locally to conduct the sophisticated statewide investigation this case appears to require. The borough police department, which has primary investigative jurisdiction over this type of case, employs only two detectives to handle the entire caseload. Were they to devote the volumes of time necessary to detect answers to these questions, they would be unavailable to spend time on other important files...
>
> ...Also I note that given participation in the investigation leading to the conclusions reached in 1987, neither department (Indiana County or IUP police) is well positioned to conduct even what appears to be an unbiased investigation..."
>
> Robert S. Bell, Indiana County District Attorney

The words were music to my ears. The document dated May 16, 1996 represented a major milestone in our six-year battle for justice. We learned many lessons along the way, the biggest, patience.

Six months later, the state deputy attorney general called to set up a meeting to discuss the case in their Pittsburgh office. No family members or attorney invited. I had to fly solo with only one week to squeeze tons of data into a concise presentation.

I worked day and night sorting and labeling evidence into chronological order. Piecing together a comprehensive outline of important facts and unanswered questions proved to be my biggest challenge. There was no room for error; everything had to be perfect.

No easy task and even harder if as you sift through boxes of documents, disturbing photographs, mounds of newspaper clippings, letters, tapes and who knows what else, you question your own competence. Fear took over a few times but the magnitude of hope this moment held for this family pushed me through every doubt.

Deep breathing exercises helped, especially the Sunday night before the big meeting. Visions of turning this complicated case over to people with incredible powers danced in my head. The state investigator had already mentioned a grand jury investigation during one of our phone conversations, which meant people would have to talk, tell the truth or face jail.

I don't know how I managed to get a wink of sleep that night but I woke up bright-eyed and bushy tailed (I love that expression), roaring and ready to go! Got dressed, managed to swallow some food, sat down to scan my notes before heading out the door, then—BANG!

No, I wasn't shot. The valve on the hot water tank exploded, shooting scalding water all over the laundry room in the house I had recently rented. Ironic, I thought, that's just how I feel right now—ready to blow!

Now this tidbit might come in handy for anyone who might encounter a similar situation. A friend told me to turn the red dial on the tank to the "vacation" setting and said it'd be fine until I got home. I snickered while turning the dial. The tank blew its top and had to be sent on "vacation." "How symbolic!" I thought while driving downtown for the meeting. Now, if I could just afford the vacation part.

My hands trembled as I walked through the door of the state attorney general's local office at ten-thirty on the morning of Monday, October 7, the day before my birthday. The receptionist ushered me into a large room and motioned towards a chair at a long conference table.

While waiting, I separated my six-inch stack of papers into smaller piles according to presentation order, uncapped the bottle of cold drinking water stuck in my purse, and set it on the table to my right. I had on heavy-duty rose-colored glasses that day. The investigator sounded enthusiastic about the case over the phone. We talked about evidence; he spoke of plans to meet with the family.

Two men dressed in suits and ties walked in about five minutes later. The deputy attorney general made introductions. We shook hands, and much to my surprise, the investigator sat down and immediately said he had already spoken to people in Indiana.

"You know your key witness has turned on you," he said. "I talked to the IUP officer and he said he never said anything about

245

the year 2010. He's done a one-eighty turn on you. He also told us we were wasting our time because we'd never find anything there."

The fact that the IUP officer said what he did was not surprising. I thought he might have been being sarcastic and even if he wasn't, would he ever admit to the comment and what it implied? Either way, what difference did it make? Did the investigation depend on what one officer said or didn't say?

His condescending attitude and combative demeanor caught me off guard. Instead of finding the safety and trust I expected, I felt my competence and integrity challenged. Of course, I'd been around the block more than once and faced worse affronts than this man dealt out. He may have rocked the boat but nothing could quiet the wind in my sails.

I did my job. I quoted facts, figures, phone numbers, theories, police reports, and every piece of information collected for years. I presented evidence and the investigator asked questions, gave opinions and tore my theories apart, which I assumed was his job. We calmly debated specifics for hours until murder entered the picture.

As soon as he began questioning the possibility of murder, I lost my cool, picked up the picture of Jack's crumbled, bloody body in the stairwell and slapped it on the table in front of him.

"Are you going to tell me this kid wasn't murdered?" I said, totally frustrated. "Look at him! Can you tell me how he ended up dead in this stairwell? Can you tell me he was drunk, walked down into that stairwell to urinate in the middle of the night and ended up dead when no alcohol was found in his body? Give me a break! How do you explain the three skull fractures?"

Just like the hot water tank earlier that morning, my safety valve blew! All of a sudden, all the pressure building inside me for weeks, months, years, let loose. I was sick and tired of explaining and defending the same evidence over and over again and again. The smirk on his face and his condescending attitude tripped the switch that lit my fuse. I had had enough and wanted to go home.

"The facts in this case have nothing to do with me!" I wanted to scream out loud but didn't. "Would anyone ever take this person's life and death seriously?"

The deputy attorney general sat quietly at the end of the table through most of the meeting, left for lunch and came back surprised we were "still at it." With a paper cup of soda in hand, he casually stood at the side of the table, leafing through the piles of paper in front of us.

"She has everything here," he said, smiling at me. "Right down to the phone numbers. I'm impressed."

"Now all you have to do is check it out," I thought but never said.

"We are putting this into capable hands," he said, placing his hand on the investigator's shoulder. "Our investigator is very familiar with IUP; that is his alma mater. He knows a lot of people up there and knows his way around."

The investigator reached across the table, hand extended, to show me the IUP class ring on his finger. For some reason, my heart sank along with my hopes. Here was a grown man, around thirty-five, still wearing his gold IUP class ring with a big red stone in the middle. Could he be objective?

With my rose-colored glasses shattered into a million pieces, I thanked them for their time and drove my weary, disillusioned, shaky body home. No matter what happened, I had done my very best and given my all that day. They said they would be in touch. Whatever. I didn't really care at this point or want to think, hear or talk about Jack's death anymore.

"Tomorrow is my birthday and I'm going to enjoy it," I thought while turning the key in my front door, then instantly remembered the water-soaked mess on the laundry room floor. First things first, I thought, picking up the phone to tell Elaine how the meeting went.

The landlord replaced the water heater early the next day. I tried my best to put on a happy face and celebrate my life that year, but felt disconnected, out of it. My sister, mom and kids, who were now adults, came for pizza, cake and ice cream. I went through the motions, and blew out my candles. The case had finally taken its toll on my heart, body, mind and spirit. I felt numb, discouraged, and exhausted to the point of total collapse.

I had no more to give. I had to let go.

# TWENTY-EIGHT

*The moral arc of the universe bends at the elbow of justice.*
　　　　　　　　　　　　　Martin Luther King, Jr.

Once the attorney general took over, I gladly stepped aside. I rang in the new year of 1997 working as a private investigator. I also earned a few dollars writing monthly articles for a couple of local special interest magazines and traveling around Pennsylvania conducting research interviews for the University of Chicago.

I can say without hesitation, after doing private investigating for almost a year, the best part of the job is watching someone's face when you tell them what you do for a living. Almost as much fun as flipping out your photo I.D. to prove it's true. That's about as glamorous as it gets, no matter what you see on television.

Most of the time, you sit in your car or somewhere else just as uncomfortable for hours, day and night, doing surveillance, watching, and waiting. You can't leave to eat, pee or get a drink of water. You learn to prepare for anything and everything before heading out on a case.

This is how it works: you get an assignment and you build a case. If a client calls at midnight and suspects her husband is at such and such motel with another woman, you're on your way, pronto. You might sit for hours hoping to catch him in the act, which is exactly what happened my first time out.

The client called and gave me directions to a motel; she suspected her husband was having an affair with another woman that afternoon. I jumped in the car immediately. You have to be on your toes day and night to do this job. I refused to carry a gun but a camera, video or otherwise, is a must.

That day, shortly after pulling into the parking lot of the suspected motel, a couple emerged from one of the many lookalike doors, holding hands. I recognized the husband from a photo in the file. Click, caught them hugging and kissing. Click. Click. Click. A few more shots for good measure, scribble down license plate numbers, head to the nearest photo lab, develop film, show my boss and voila! Case closed.

"You got pictures on your first time out! That's great," he said, sounding very pleased. "You don't usually have this kind of luck on this type of case."

I smiled, pretty proud of myself, while dialing the phone to call my client. She wanted to meet right away in the parking lot of a nearby Kentucky Fried Chicken. We described our cars. Ten minutes later, I pulled into the lot, and backed into a space to watch for her.

She looked to be in her late twenties as she stepped out of the car, turned around, opened the back door, unlatched one child's car seat belt, reached across the back seat to unlatch another; then picked a baby up out of the car seat closest to her, grabbed the toddler's hand and headed towards my car.

"Asshole!" I thought, thinking of her husband off cavorting with another woman while his wife cared for the two children they created together. "This is going to break her heart."

Even though she paid to know the truth, I hated showing her pictures of her husband groping another woman in broad daylight in a motel parking lot following their secret rendezvous. She stood next to my car staring at the incriminating evidence, tears streaming down both cheeks, kids fussing. "Thanks," she said, turning towards her car.

"This job sucks!" I thought, watching her strap the kids back into their car seats, then get behind the wheel and drive off. My only satisfaction came from imagining his stunned face as she shoved the pictures under his nose at the dinner table. Oh, to be a fly on the wall that night!

Believe me, the infidelity cases sucked. My boss was right. You might sit waiting and watching for hours, days, weeks and come up empty-handed. Boring! Try sitting on a bar stool for eight hours—of course you can't get drunk and stupid on the job—watching to see if a suspected bartender pockets money out of the cash register. Even more boring, if at all possible, is sitting in front of someone's house in your car for hours, waiting to catch them going to work or doing strenuous activity while collecting disability.

I finally refused assignments that involved tailing strangers after one guy caught on and doubled back on me in the middle of the night. He turned into a used car lot, circled around, pulled out behind my car and started following me! I sped away, turning up different streets, terrified and then relieved when he finally veered off in another direction. He scared the living hell out of me but I didn't quit. Interesting cases, such as recording witness depositions for a discrimination lawsuit and searching for an abducted child, kept me on the job, eager to do my best for my clients.

The six-year-old, who lived with his grandmother, had been taken from her front yard during a Fourth of July family picnic. She suspected her daughter and son-in-law, both on drugs, wanted to use the child to collect welfare and food stamps. Emotions ran high; the couple supposedly desperate, the grandmother angry, scared and vengeful.

Based on tips, she sent me racing off to homeless shelters, seedy motels and various other shady hangouts at all hours day and night to find her grandson. Nothing deterred me. Being a grandmother myself, I knew I'd move heaven and earth to protect my grandchildren. Plus, the situation didn't sound safe for any child.

No matter what time she called day or night with new information, I sprang into action. So, of course, I didn't hesitate when the phone rang at two in the morning. I scribbled down a few notes, splashed cold water on my face and headed out the door. I spent several sleepless nights looking for the child and didn't want to let the grandmother down.

She heard they might be staying in a trailer park about fifty miles south of Pittsburgh. Following directions, I turned onto the pitch black, narrow, two-lane country road next to the trailer park sign, cut the headlights, drove a few more feet, then stopped a good distance away from the only trailer sitting in the middle of a vast, moonlit field.

Slowly, quietly, I inched the car door open, gingerly placing my foot in the tall, dry, brittle, weedy grass. Crunch. Crunch. Crunch. Crunch. Each footstep broke the silence and sounded even louder the closer I came to the shiny silver trailer parked in the middle of nowhere.

"Are you crazy?" the voice in my head whispered as I nervously placed a foot down beneath the trailer's only lit window. "Someone's going to blow your damn head off! Who'd know? Get the hell out of here!"

Man, did I make tracks! I didn't care who heard me running as fast as my legs could carry me back to my car. I turned the key in the ignition, hit the lights and got the hell out of there! Of course, not telling the client you nearly peed your pants is also part of the job. "No results," was the official finding recorded in the case file. However, "No more traipsing around deserted trailer parks in the dark, ever again!" became permanently etched in my brain under the heading: Life Lessons.

"Have you heard anything from your daughter?" I asked my client, after thinking the situation over for several hours before contacting her around noon the next day.

"Yes, she called a few times asking for money," the woman said, anger rising in her voice. "I told her no and to bring my grandson back!"

"What do you think about trying a different approach?" I said, realizing that chasing her daughter all over creation was not working. "Do you remember the old adage, 'You catch more flies with honey than vinegar?' Well, the next time she calls, talk nice, act concerned for her well being, make her believe you're on her side and want to help. What do you think?"

"It's not going to be easy but I'll try," she said. "I don't think it will work, though."

Two days later, she held her grandson safely in her arms. Her daughter took the bait—hook, line and sinker. Plus, she agreed to leave the child for a visit. My client immediately contacted her attorney and filed for full custody the next day. She then hired me to serve her daughter. I knocked on the door of this run-down motel, the girl answered, verified her name, and I quickly shoved the court papers hidden behind my back into her hand.

She jerked back, lifted her leg and kicked me in the stomach with all her might! Talk about a tough job!

A few days later, the client invited me to her house for a cookout to show her appreciation and to meet her grandson. My boss said the client was very pleased with my work and encouraged me to go. Accepting her invitation felt awkward but I really did want to meet the little boy I'd searched for night and day for almost a month.

"This is the lady who looked everywhere for you," the grandmother said to the small brown-haired boy sitting cross-legged on a plush, beige living room chair playing with a toy.

"I know," he said, calmly looking up at me with big brown eyes. "I saw you. I saw you looking for me."

I resigned the next day. What if something horrible had happened to him as I drove around driving myself crazy looking for him? My nerves were shot. I decided to find a less heart-wrenching job, and dare I say, more cheerful? I continued writing, conducted research interviews when needed and started my own business in my spare time.

Of course, I checked in with Elaine, John or Marisa every once in awhile to see if anyone heard from the state attorney general. Months passed. Not a word, not even the expected request to meet with the family and their attorney. No grand jury. Nothing. Again, all you can do is wait. Our last contact that summer was when I called to ask Marisa for her delicious broccoli salad recipe, so I could make it for the fourth of July.

"I'm surprised you remember my broccoli salad," Marisa said. "It's really simple to make. All you do is mix one to one and a half bunches of finely chopped broccoli, one pound of bacon crumbled, a half onion chopped and a cup of cheddar cheese.

"I love your broccoli salad," I said, "How is everybody doing?"

"We're all fine," she said. "What do you think's happening?

"No clue," I replied. "I just wonder why you guys haven't heard from them yet."

"It doesn't matter," Marisa said. "As long as they're investigating his death, right? Here, let me give you the rest of the recipe. This is the dressing: mix it in a separate bowl and add it to the broccoli right before you eat. Use one cup of Hellmann's mayonnaise—it won't taste the same if you use any other kind—two tablespoons of white vinegar and a half-cup of sugar. Remember, put the dressing on just before you eat or it'll get soggy."

We talked again a couple of weeks before Thanksgiving following my call to the state attorney general's office. A year had passed since our meeting and I constantly wondered why the investigator never contacted the family or convened a grand jury, as mentioned. Of course, talking myself into placing the call took hours but getting answers only minutes.

"Did you see the video tape from the second autopsy?" the investigator in the state attorney general's office said sounding angry, which confused me. "The one the Indiana County Coroner made?"

"No, I never saw it," I said, wondering why he sounded as if I did something wrong.

"Well, you better," he said. "If I'd a known about that tape, I never would have rode this horse so long!"

"Okay," I said, caught totally off guard by his hostile demeanor. "I can get a copy..."

"You better get a copy! Wecht said the kid fell! He created a reasonable doubt. Do you know what that means?" the investigator said, pausing. "It means no one can ever be indicted for this kid's murder."

"I can't believe it!" I said, shocked.

"Well, believe it," he replied. "And, I strongly suggest you get a copy of that tape!"

I immediately contacted the family's attorney, explained what just happened and asked if he had a copy of the second autopsy tape. He did, so I made plans to pick it up the next day.

"I really don't think you want to watch it," he said. "It's very disturbing."

"I have to," I said, swallowing my fear. "I have to see what the investigator's talking about. It's important."

As was mentioned before, I was so relieved to find the little cassette tape under the larger videotape in the bottom of the big, brown envelope the family's attorney handed me. I don't know how I could have handled watching his body being sawed into pieces in color on television in my living room. Just listening to the sound of the electric saw cutting through his bones ripped my heart to pieces.

Looking back now, I wonder why this part of the story was not leaked to the media. Maybe we didn't know what to make of all this at the time. Dr. Wecht presented several possible scenarios concerning Jack's death. Isn't that what forensic experts do? How could Wecht just *saying* Jack fell create a reasonable doubt?

Forensic experts testify in murder cases all the time and often present opposing and contradictory opinions. Does the murderer go free because one expert testifies the victim fell, and another says he was bludgeoned to death with a baseball bat? Don't other factors such as evidence and circumstances come into play? I called Dr. Wecht to tell him what happened.

"I didn't know it was being taped," he said.

Has this ever happened before?" I asked. "Have you ever been involved in a case where..."

He cut me short at that point and told me to draw up a list of questions and send it in the mail, which I did but never received back. That was the last time we spoke.

I called Elaine, then John, with the devastating news.

"Where do we go from here?" John said, along with a few choice red-faced words.

"I don't know, John," I said, deflated. "I really don't know."

I couldn't help but wonder why Wecht said he didn't know he was being taped. Didn't he see Streams holding a camera in front of his face during the autopsy? Was it a hidden camera? Surely the coroner asked permission to film the procedure, right? You have to ask permission to tape a conversation, so it stands to reason you'd have to do the same with a video camera—especially in this situation.

I realize now the family let go at this point. They never called Wecht to discuss what happened, or even their own attorney. No response. They took the major blow quietly on the chin. What else could they do? How many times can you let high hopes shatter your heart? They either had to throw in the towel or keep bleeding.

Three years later, I bumped into Elaine coming out of a movie theater with a friend at a local shopping center. We hugged, exchanged pleasantries, and then she told me the news.

"I've been meaning to call you," she said, sounding light and airy. "A retired Indiana Borough police officer called Wecht's office and left a message. They called and told Lisa. He said something about Jack coming to him for protection. Call Lisa. She can tell you."

"I will," I said, stunned by the implications of the message. A police officer said Jack came to him for protection—from whom? Seems to me, the answer to that one question would answer them all. Right?

I raced home and called Lisa for more details.

"He said he is a retired Indiana Borough police officer," she said reading and spelling his name. "He said Jack came to him for protection two weeks before his death."

Let me see, if he considered the day his body was found on October 21 the day of his death, two weeks would be October 7 or one day after the major drug bust in Indiana on October 6. Once again, I grabbed straws. I called the Indiana Borough police station to verify his identity, then called information to find an address and phone number. No listing.

So, I did the next best thing. I hired a private investigator, who had the information the next day. I dialed his number, no answer. I contacted Elaine, gave her the number. We both called for days. No response. Finally, I suggested she write a letter asking him to please tell her about his meeting with her son.

I'd like to say he could not refuse the pleas of a mother desperate to find out who killed her son and why, but that's not what happened. Apparently, just like everyone else, he didn't want involved. Who knows? Maybe he called to unburden his conscience or, if you happen to be looking through rose-colored glasses, to let the family know—once and for all—Jack was murdered and knew exactly who kill him.

Even if the state attorney general—or even the president of the United States for that matter—says no one can ever be indicted for Jack's murder, does that take away this family's need to know the truth about what happened to their loved one?

As for the retired Indiana Borough police officer, there's only one word for him: "Coward." And the big question is: "Why didn't you *protect* him?"

# TWENTY-NINE

*To see your drama clearly is to be liberated from it.*
                                    CHINESE FORTUNE COOKIE

Elaine and I talked about ways around this latest development. I also asked her what she thought about filing a complaint against Dr. Griffin to have his medical license revoked in Pennsylvania. She thought it was a good idea, so I sent to the state licensing board for procedure information.

We met for lunch at a restaurant near her office on March 28, 2000. We had eaten there many times over the years to discuss the case. This time, I handed her complaint forms to fill out along with specifics details pertaining to Dr. Griffin's medical opinions in this case. And explained the papers had to be notarized before sending them to the state for investigation.

"I can't believe it's been thirteen years since Jack died," she said between bites of hot turkey sandwich, mashed potatoes and gravy. "I still keep hoping someone will walk up to me someday and say, 'I know what happened to your son.'"

"You are very brave," I said, sharing her hope. "I don't think I could have endured what you've been through over the past thirteen years. Sometimes I feel so bad about dragging you through all of this and there's still no answer."

Her eyes looked at me but her mind seemed somewhere else.

"Did you ever think when you heard my voice on the phone, 'What does this woman want now?' Did you ever want me to go away? Would you tell me if you did?"

Everything burning in my chest since day one came pouring out. "I've always feel like I am hurting you every time I call," I said, tears filling my eyes. "I've always felt so bad about it all. I've imagined seeing through your eyes many times and can only guess how much pain this has caused you over the years."

"Why did you say that to me?" she said, interrupting. "Why did you say I was brave? I always felt like I had my head in the sand. I've always felt like I should have done more. I still feel that way."

I listened. She had a lot on her chest, too.

"I dealt with this the only way I know how to deal with my son's death," she said, looking down at her plate. "At the time, I could barely deal with anything. Even now, I sometimes wonder if I've dealt with it."

She took a sip of water.

"I could have never done what you did," she said, moving her head slowly back and forth. "I wouldn't have even known where to begin. You knew how to put it all together and you knew what to do. I am thankful for what you have done. I never blamed you. I'm on your side."

A few weeks later, I sent Elaine, John, and Jack, Sr. letters with the retired Indiana Borough police officer's information including directions to his house. If they wanted to talk to him and find out who probably killed Jack, I'd be more than happy to go with them.

Shortly afterwards, Elaine called about something—perhaps the letter, I can't remember—and said she didn't have time to fill out the complaint against Dr. Griffin.

"It's up to you," I said, realizing the time had come to leave the ball in their court and let them decide what to do with it.

No one ever asked me to go with them to talk with the retired police officer; I often wonder what he might have said about his meeting with Jack. I've also wondered if the officer told fellow officers about Jack asking for police protection.

What do you think the chances are that he mentioned his encounter with Jack to other officers once the Missing Persons report was filed? Did the subject come up during roll call or even normal conversation in the police station? "Hey, that's the same kid that came to me two weeks ago asking for protection from so and so." Did Detective Sergeant Antolik, the investigator in this case, hear about Jack's request from his fellow officer or through the precinct grapevine?

When Antolik kept telling the press he believed Jack was "abducted" or "kidnapped," was he the only one making an educated guess based on information Jack provided Indiana Borough Police before his death?

And why weren't these distraught parents—desperate to find their son—told he came to them for protection the minute they stepped foot in their police station?

# THIRTY

*Human progress is neither automatic nor inevitable.... Every step towards the goal of justice required sacrifice, suffering and struggle; the tireless exertions and passionate concern of dedicated individuals.*

Martin Luther King, Jr.

Fast-forward, November 2004. A childhood acquaintance called after forty years to say hello and catch up. Forty years! Our parents were lifelong friends. She married, had grown children, and much to my surprised lived less than two miles away from the house where I raised my kids in Penn Hills.

Strange our paths never crossed at the local supermarket in all those years. Would we have recognized each other? We may have walked past each other several times and not known it. Even stranger was how similar our lives turned out to be. We were both divorced and running our own small businesses. She co-owned a tree service with her son. I now published a countywide entertainment newspaper and was writing my first book.

"What's it about?" she asked.

As soon as the words, "The kid in the stairwell up at IUP," came out of my mouth, she recalled the story.

"That was the kid who choked to death on his own vomit, right? That was strange. That's why I remember. So what happened?"

I shared a few details, told her what the state attorney general said and left it at that. No sense reliving the nightmare with her or anyone else for that matter.

"I might know someone who can help," she said, mentioning a former FBI agent she knew. "I'll give him a call. Maybe he'll talk to you."

"Sure, that'd be great," I said, not giving too much weight to her words. My goal after fifteen years was to tell the world about what happened to this college student and his family. Any hope of solving the case vanished years ago, more specifically, at the exact moment the state attorney general said no one could ever be indicted for Jack's murder.

We planned to meet for lunch before Christmas, if we could, and promised to touch base before then.

"Why is this person trying to reconnect with me now," I wondered. "I can't even remember what she looks like." We must have been around six or seven years old the last time we saw each other and weren't even close back then. Her sudden and persistent desire to see me again felt odd. Our polite agreement to meet was soon forgotten; life before the holidays is too hectic to get involved with any of this right now.

True to her word, however, she called back two weeks before Christmas. She had contacted the former FBI agent and wanted to set up a date and time for us to meet with him and another person she knew from the Federal Aviation Administration (FAA).

"Why would I want to meet someone from the Federal Aviation Administration?" I asked. "What's he got to do with any of this?"

"He does private investigations," she said. "Just talk to him. Is Tuesday good for you? He flies around a lot but he'll be in Pittsburgh that day. We can meet somewhere near the airport."

I agreed, knowing full well no one was hiring a private investigator—but her persistence and enthusiasm won me over.

"It's all set," she said, when she called back a few minutes later. "One o'clock, Tuesday, Bruegger's Bagels on Green Tree Road. Do you know where that is?"

"Yes," I said, still unsure about getting involved in the case again. "Next Tuesday, one o'clock, Bruegger's Bagels, Green Tree Road."

"I can't wait to see you!" she said, elated.

"It'll be great," I said, trying to match her enthusiasm, while dealing with the prospect of dredging up all the morbid details for the umpteenth time for two complete strangers right before the holidays.

Early Tuesday morning, I cancelled, claiming an upset stomach. Perhaps just the thought of regurgitating this story one more time for one more person who could do nothing made me feel sick.

"Are you sure?" she said, very disappointed. I felt guilty.

"Why don't you give them my phone number," I said, figuring this would end her good intentions. "Tell them I want to talk to them but can't today."

"Hello," a deep male voice said when I picked up the phone later that afternoon. "Joanne told me you're not feeling well. I thought I'd give you a call so we can talk." It was the guy from the FAA. Great.

"What's this all about," he said, fishing for details. I had no problem reciting the facts of the case for the zillionth time. We talked for over two hours. He listened, asked some questions, and then offered his opinion.

"The reason you can't get the answers you seek is because you don't have the power," he said. "You have no power behind you to find the truth. No one has to answer your questions or tell you anything. Now, if someone from the FBI asks questions, you better answer. See what I mean? You answer, tell the truth, or go to jail for five years."

He was absolutely right! Here I was running around begging for justice with no power to demand answers. Of course, I knew deep inside what he said was true years ago but his words validated my feelings and made my ongoing struggle appear crystal clear. All these years, I'd been searching for someone with power to help this family. I talked with lawyers, district attorneys, police, and the deputy state attorney general—anyone who'd listen. I even called the FBI in the beginning and the agent told me Jack's murder did not fall under federal jurisdiction.

The case, as they put it, had to cross state lines to be classified as a federal crime. That door closed long ago, so what did this guy think he was going to do to get this case to the federal level? It all seemed hopeless to me.

"I know someone in the U.S. Attorney's office," he said. "I think I can set up a meeting for you. Put together a synopsis of your case. If you want me to, I'll look over it before making the appointment."

I almost fell off my chair. A chance to present the case to a U.S. Attorney! Santa arrived early that Christmas with the best present of all!

"Put it together and give me a call," he said, rattling off his cell phone number.

"Thank you," I said more than once before hanging up, and the room began to spin.

"At the least, it sounds like a civil rights violation to me," he said.

"Joe," I said a few minutes after the enormity of this task set in. "I hate to ask, because I don't want to sound ungrateful, but can we plan to meet after the holidays? I don't think I can handle all this right now."

"I'm not going anywhere," he said in a calm, reassuring voice. "We'll plan to meet whenever you're ready."

I couldn't believe it! This woman calls after forty years and ends up giving me a chance to present this case to the United States Justice Department! I called everyone: my family, Jack's family, and friends. I wanted to shout from the rooftop. "A Christmas miracle, that's what this is," I thought, my rose-colored glasses working overtime. I would present this case to the highest power in the land! My cup runneth over.

Of course, waiting until after Christmas flew right out the window. The next day, I sat down at the computer and outlined the case in chronological order, point-by-point, single-spaced. Fourteen years of work had to be squeezed into two pages in two days.

"I realize you're probably busy with the holidays," I said, calling him, too excited to wait another minute past fifteen years.

"Let me call you back to see what I can do," he said, surprised.

I felt so stupid minutes after placing the call. I couldn't help it. He offered to make my dream come true. I wanted the appointment now. I also needed to know if this guy was real. As you know, my high hopes crashed and burned many, many times.

He called the day before Christmas Eve and again expressed his surprise over my eagerness to get started. He'd be in town the Monday after Christmas—Christmas fell on Saturday that year—and promised to call to set up a meeting. We met Tuesday morning in front of a Target superstore near the airport. From there, we moved to a nearby restaurant to discuss my outline over a cup of coffee.

He was tall, over six feet, with broad shoulders, deep blue eyes and as bald as a billiard ball. He looked like an ex-state trooper and later confirmed he was. He dressed completely in black: black trench coat and black felt Fedora. He looked as if he had just stepped off the silver screen. A stereotypical private detective if ever I saw one. As he talked, he ran his hand over the top of his clean-shaven head. I listened quietly as he recalled other cases, and for some reason, said something about replacing an engine in a car as a teen. He also mentioned the book he had just published and offered a few unsolicited details.

I sipped on a glass of ice tea, trying not to fidget, waiting for the opportunity to discuss my outline. On his second cup of coffee, we got down to business. He scanned the outline, mentioned his connection to the U.S. attorney's office again and promised to get back to me with proposed revisions in a few days.

I tried not to look ahead, but visions of sitting down to discuss Jack's murder with the U.S. attorney danced in my head right into 2005. Days turned into weeks, however, but he never called—the New Year started out with a bang! Persistent, I called until he finally picked up.

He was busy, he said. As a matter of fact, he was in a meeting in the U.S. Attorney's office as we spoke. He promised to call back. I thought he meant that day. A week later, again after several attempts, he answered the phone in his now too busy to talk tone of voice. He suggested changing the outline around in a few places, to emphasize certain points and eliminate others.

"Do you have this on your computer?" he asked. "E-mail me the changes and we'll go from there."

"I'll try," I said, explaining my inept ability to email anything on my new computer. After several failed attempts, I had to offer to send it the old-fashioned way, through the mail. He sounded put out as he recited his address. I immediately drove to the post office and sent the revised outline on its way.

Weeks passed, no word. I hated to bother him again but saw no alternative.

"I never got it," he said. I repeated the address he gave me. The street was misspelled. So, I ran another copy off the computer and dashed to the post office.

That was it! I never heard from the tough-talking, big wheel Private Dick again, no matter how many times I called. Twice he answered, promised to call back, but never did. Another major let down or so it seemed—until a waitress in a Chinese restaurant where my mother and I ate lunch a few weeks later set a new perspective down in front of me on the table in the form of a fortune cookie.

Crack.

# THIRTY-ONE

*Don't wait for others to open doors for you.*
CHINESE FORTUNE COOKIE

I had to laugh. Funny, how the universe seems to find a way to tell you exactly what you need to hear when you need to hear it. I didn't need bald-headed Kojak, minus the lollypop, or anyone else to make an appointment with the U.S. attorney for me; I'd do it myself. Why not? All they can say is, no. Big deal—I've heard the word before and can live with it.

On April 18, 2005, I picked up the phone, called the U.S. Attorney's office in Pittsburgh and asked for the address. I'd send an outline through the mail with hopes someone would read it and become intrigued enough to contact me.

After stating my purpose and offering a brief explanation, the receptionist took my name and number then said someone would get back to me. Two days later, a public relations director for the U.S. attorney returned my call. She listened to the circumstances surrounding my request and promised to call back with an answer as soon as possible. Another two days passed; she kept her word and provided the answer I expected to hear. The case did not fall under the jurisdiction of the U.S. attorney.

"You have to go to local authorities," she said. "U.S. attorneys usually work in conjunction with other law enforcement agencies."

"I've already been to the district attorney, the state attorney general, there is no place else to go with this case. The state attorney general said no one can be indicted for this kid's murder because of something Dr. Cyril Wecht said," I blurted the words out not realizing a few of them were magic. "Can I at least send in a synopsis of this case for someone to look at? Maybe the U.S. attorney can tell us what to do next. Please."

"I'll talk to them and call you back," she said.

"That's all I ask," I said. "Thank you."

Send it; bring it, whatever it takes. At least I could say I did my best to get it to the top of the ladder, the last rung on the judicial ladder. The end. I thought for sure she'd call Friday but when Marisa called out of the blue Monday night, I still hadn't heard from the woman at the U.S. Attorney's office.

"How's it going?" she asked. "Anything ever happen with the U.S. attorney?"

"Might as well forget it," I said, feeling defeat once again. "They're not going to do anything, Marisa. They only work on cases with other law enforcement agencies."

"Oh," she said, her voice now as disappointed as mine. We chatted, catching up on news but all I could focus on was how I failed them once again.

That night, I fell asleep, wondering what to do next and woke up angry. "I could use a little help here!" I said, staring up at the ceiling. I shoved back the covers, stomped out of bed and down the stairs, brushed my teeth, and picked up the phone.

The same woman at the U.S. Attorney's office picked up the phone, "Hello Margaret, this is Marlene," I said, determined to get a name and address and send the outline this time, no matter what! "I'm calling to..."

"I'm glad you called," she said. "An agent at the FBI wants to talk to you. Here's his name and number. He's expecting your call."

I stopped breathing. My heart pounded loudly in my ears, almost drowning out her voice as she recited the information. An FBI agent wanted to talk to me? He was expecting my call? My hands and feet turned to ice. I shivered.

"Thank you," I said, staring at his name as I picked up the phone, pushed a few buttons, hung up and paced back and forth across the kitchen floor.

"Walk through the fear," I said out loud. "You have to walk through the fear." I sat back down on the couch, took a couple of very long, deep breaths, and then slowly pushed the numbered buttons on the phone.

As soon as we introduced ourselves and he asked about the case, I took off, spouting details without coming up for air. The agent listened and only interrupted to clarify one thing, "Cyril Wecht was not the county coroner when he acted in this case. Is that correct?"

"No, he was retained by the family," I replied, suddenly recalling the FBI was investigating Dr. Wecht. I forgot about seeing FBI agents carrying files and computers out of his office on the local news several weeks before.

Dr. Wecht served as Allegheny County Coroner for several years before and after working on this case. I had no idea why he was under investigation and was not about to ask. My heart sank and I might have even moaned at some point. For the record, the case against Dr. Wecht was dismissed.

"It sounds like you might want to talk to another agent who deals with Indiana County," he said. "Here's the number. It sounds like a political corruption case, to me. See what they say."

"Alright," I said, hand shaking as I jotted down the number.

I took another deep breath, dialed again. A woman answered and identified herself as the complaint officer. I told her about my conversation with the other agent.

"Would you like to make an appointment or send in the complaint?" she asked.

"Make an appointment?" I said, caught off guard.

"I'll switch you to the supervisor," she said. "Leave your name and number. He'll get back to you."

I left my name and number along with the name of the agent who referred me to his office, hung up, and sat staring into space. "I just made an appointment with the Federal Bureau of Investigation," I said out loud to no one, but my stomach heard and did a few flips before total panic set in. I grabbed the phone and called back.

"I changed my mind. I'd rather send the complaint," I said as calmly as possible.

"That's fine," she said. "Here's the address."

As soon as I started writing, my body stopped trembling. Actually, I felt elated! Just drop it in the mail. That's it! I did it! "Yes! Yes!" I shouted arms stretched up in the air over my head in victory. I did it! I did it! I felt like a prizefighter in the ring prancing around in victory. Now, all I had to do was stuff everything in an envelope and send it away!

Right in the middle of my euphoria, the phone rang.

"Hello, is this Marlene?" the male voice asked before identifying himself as an FBI agent. "I understand you'd like to set up an appointment."

Caught off guard, I didn't know what to say.

"I thought I'd send the information instead," I said hoping to end the conversation.

"Is there a reason you don't want to talk to me in person?" he asked.

"No, I just thought it's a lot of information so it'd be better if I send everything so you could look at it yourself," I said, instead of saying, "I'm scared to death!"

"I'd like to meet with you," he said. "I can meet you in Indiana."

"No!" I replied, more emphatic than necessary.

"Do you know where the Pittsburgh office is?" he asked. "Do you want to come there?"

"Well," I said, hesitating. I didn't want to go anywhere except to the bathroom and throw up my guts at that moment.

"I could come to your house," he said. "How does Thursday around twelve-thirty sound?"

"Okay," I said. "That way I don't have to pack everything up and carry it."

"Then I'll see you at twelve-thirty Thursday," he said. "What's the address?"

It was over, done. The FBI was coming to my house in two days. Shaking, I slowly put the phone down. Now, not only did I have to pull fifteen years of stuff together into an understandable and concise case—I had to clean the house!

I had to pinch myself as I picked up the phone to tell Jack's family as well as my own about the strange turn of events. This was it. I had to get ready.

"What do you mean you have to get ready?" John said. "You've been preparing for fifteen years!"

"Can you believe it, John? We made it!" I said to the man who had told me his heart-wrenching story those many years ago. We'd been through so much together on our quest for the truth. For the first time since we met, he sobbed.

"It's all right," I said softly, tears filling my own eyes. "It's going to be alright."

"I'm sorry," he said. "I just can't help it."

I knew exactly how he felt but could not let emotions get the better of me this late in the game. Focusing on putting together the best presentation of my life in two days now my main objective. I'd be ready. I was ready. I could spit out every detail of this case in my sleep. I'd been waiting for so long and didn't know it.

"This sounds like your last stop," the FBI agent said the first time we spoke, and at that exact moment I realized it was true. I mean, if you can't find justice at the U.S. Justice Department, what's next?

I unfolded the legs on my old blue vinyl-top card table, set it up in the middle of my small living room, then started sorting all the papers into piles.

I checked the chronological outline of events I'd put together to present to the U.S. Attorney, went through all the documents, and labeled each one to match corresponding letters and numbers on the two-page outline. I also had the comprehensive and well-organized notebook of evidence prepared by the family's attorney. I was ready to go. Nervous? Definitely. Anxious, you bet! But if anyone was ready for this moment, it was me.

I spent all day Wednesday arranging items in order on the card table. We'd be a little cramped for space but there was enough room for two chairs and this would have to do. Tomorrow afternoon an FBI agent would knock on my door. There was lot of ground to cover, explain, present and cram into whatever time he'd give me.

The video of the family on the local talk show sat prompted in the VCR ready to run, the *Unsolved Mysteries* tape close at hand. A pile of duplicate documents neatly piled on the table in front of his designated chair directly opposite mine. I didn't think I'd be able to sleep at all that night but managed to get a few winks before waking up around eight in a total state of panic.

What if he wanted to take all my documents? I'd have to give him everything; I rushed downstairs to make sure there were copies of everything.

Extra copies of the toxicology report and original autopsy were missing. I threw on a pair of jeans and a T-shirt drove to a nearby copy machine, grabbed a bacon, egg and cheese biscuit at McDonald's, and then raced back home.

Whew! My heart was racing a mile a minute as I searched my closet for something decent to wear. Not formal but professional black pants, magenta top, black shoes. I never wear shoes in the house—must remember—absolute must.

Around noon, I checked my pulse because my heart felt as if someone was beating one of those great big drums—like in a parade—right inside my chest. Boom! Boom! Boom! My head felt light and I had to keep taking deep breaths to calm myself. I wasn't afraid, just anxious. Everything had to be perfect; this was the last stop at the end of a very long journey.

I popped a calming meditation CD in the stereo, pushed play, and sat on the floor with my eyes closed, trying to get a grip, twenty more minutes.

"He's coming to help," I said, breathing in. "He's not coming to confront you," I said, breathing out. "He's coming to help," breathe in. "He's friend, not foe," breathe out. "This time will be different." I glance at the clock, only minutes before twelve-thirty.

I didn't count how many times I climbed the steps to the second floor to peer out the front window. The minutes dragged; he was five, ten, twenty minutes late. Now it was almost one. He forgot, changed his mind or maybe his eleven o'clock meeting ran late. I stared at the clock, wringing my hands at one-thirty. He wasn't going to show. Finally, after arguing with myself for ten more minutes, I called his office to find out what happened.

"Let me get him on his cell phone," his secretary said. "I know he planned to meet with you."

She called right back. "He's leaving his meeting now. He should be there any minute."

Twenty more agonizing minutes of sheer torture passed before a big black truck-like vehicle with dark tinted windows pulled up and parked across the street in my neighbor's driveway.

My first thought was to tell him he couldn't park there, but I wasn't about to tell the FBI where they could park. Let my neighbor tell him. They love to tell everyone where to park and move their cars. I laughed picturing my neighbor asking him to move his car and the agent pulling out his FBI badge. I'd have paid to see the look on his face!

I leaned out the side door, greeted him and directed him down the cement steps on the side of my house. He slid a black wallet-like case out of the inside pocket of his jacket as he came towards me, then extended his hand to display his credentials. Once inside, we shook hands. I pointed to a chair and offered him something to drink, which he politely refused.

As he apologized for being late due to a nearby construction detour, I slid pictures of Jack's body in the stairwell, one black-and-white and the other in color, out of a large brown envelope and placed them on the table in front of him.

"It's hard to know where to begin," I said. "Jack was found in a stairwell at IUP. He was missing for five days. An autopsy was performed at Indiana Hospital the next day. The coroner ruled his death accidental. He said Jack was highly intoxicated, walked into the stairwell to urinate and choked to death on his own vomit."

"Where did all the blood come from?" he asked, examining the pictures. "That is blood, isn't it?"

"Yes," I replied. "And no alcohol was detected in his blood at the time of death."

He studied the toxicology report and chronological outline of events. Then for two hours, he picked items listed on the outline, asked for explanations and to see specific documents.

I felt confident and truly appreciated his respectful and professional manner. When I told him what the investigator in the state attorney general's office said about never being able to indict anyone for Jack's murder because Dr. Wecht supposedly created a reasonable doubt during the second autopsy, he shook his head.

"That's just not true," he said. "You can indict a ham sandwich. That's just an expression, of course."

He asked why it took so long for me to contact the FBI. I told him about reaching out to them years ago but was told Jack's murder did not fall under federal jurisdiction.

"I feel sorry for this family. They may never have closure," he said. "We have so many complaints about corruption. There's corruption everywhere. People don't realize right now our main focus is on terrorism."

"I'm just so happy you're here and you listened to me," I said, my face aglow. As he walked back up the steps on the side of my house, without thinking I put my hands together, looked up at the sky and said, "Thank you, thank you, thank you." A feeling of pure joy filled my heart. I understood Jack's murder still did not fall under federal jurisdiction but no matter what happened or didn't happen, my part was over.

That evening, I called John for the last time. "It's over, John," I said, explaining how the meeting went and what the FBI agent said about everything.

"I will never be able to repay you for what you've done," he said. "When no one cared and no one listened, you did. No matter what happened and no matter how they tried to stop us, you never quit. Thank you. I'll never forget what you did for my family and Jack."

"John, I hope with all my heart someday you find out who killed your brother and why. You know this started out being about Jack, but what's happened to your family over the years is as big an issue as who killed him and why. I always felt if I stopped fighting, we'd all lose. I believe with all my heart and soul that your family deserves to know the truth and has every right to want justice."

Looking back now, I realize that no matter the outcome of our painful and scary, but always courageous quest, we have lived the *real* American dream.

# THIRTY-TWO

*We should do every thing we can do to make sure
our country lives up to our children's expectations.*

Barack Obama

"Are you all ready for your first day at kindergarten?" I said to my five-year-old granddaughter, catching her on the phone early in the morning before she left for school.

"Yes," she said in her wondrous new-to-the-planet voice.

"You're going to do all kinds of new things like paste, color, sing songs," I said, still remembering my first day at "big girl" school those many years ago. "Are you excited?"

"Yes, my friends will be there," she said, rattling off the names of kids from her preschool class to prove it.

"Sounds like you're going to have a wonderful time," I said, hearing her mother's voice in the background telling her it's time to leave. "You better get going. You don't want to be late. I love you!"

"I love you, too, Grandma," she said, eager to hang up now.

Five days later while sitting around the table after dinner at my son's house, I casually asked her, "So, how do you like kindergarten so far?"

"I like it a lot!" she said, not offering details freely.

"What's your favorite part?" I said, expecting her to answer painting or even playing in the schoolyard with the other kids at recess.

"The *Pledge of Allegiance*," she said without hesitation.

"The *Pledge of Allegiance*?" I replied, looking at my daughter-in-law with a gigantic question mark on my face.

"You better believe it," her mother said, rolling her eyes. "She came home the first day and drove me crazy until she learned every word that night. She said it over and over again until she got it right."

"You can say the *Pledge of Allegiance* all by yourself?" I said, looking at her amazed. "Do you want to show me?"

She pushed her chair back from the table and walked towards me with a very serious and determined look on her young angelic face. I turned sideways in my chair away from the table. She stood directly in front of me and placed her tiny right hand in the middle of her chest over her heart.

"*I pledge allegiance to the flag of the United States of America and to the Republic for which it stands, one nation under God, indivisible, with liberty and justice for all.*"

No worries people. We're in good hands.

# EPILOGUE

*The dead add their strength and counsel to the living.*

HOPI PROVERB

I had a dream a few nights ago that felt so real. Jack was sitting to my left at a table smiling. He looked healthy, happy, content and serene. A lightness of being surrounded him, white, calm, soothing.

In contrast, my being felt full of worry, stress, hopelessness, guilt, and failure.

"I know," he said smiling sweetly. "I know the truth. We've always known the truth."

As he spoke, I felt released. All tension vanished instantly. I understood completely. "That's right," I said, nodding my head and feeling foolish for not realizing all along. How, when and where this story ends is not up to me and never was.

# AUTHOR'S NOTE

To the best of my knowledge the renegade Sig Tau fraternity no longer functions in Indiana. According to a former student who now works for the university's student life department, the group disbanded years ago.

"I was a student here back in the early 90's and everyone knew they were bad news and to stay away from them," she said over the phone the other day. "The new Sigma Tau Gamma fraternity earned back their national charter in 2001 and are again recognized by the university."

If you have any questions, comments or information concerning this case please contact me anytime at *www.marlene-gentilcore.com.*

*Marlene Gentilcore*
*October 21, 2010*

# NOTES

**CHAPTER ONE**
Jack Alan Davis, Jr. Second Autopsy Video, Indiana County Coroner, Streams, Thomas, November 13, 1990

**CHAPTER FOUR**
"Student Missing," *Indiana Gazette*, (Indiana, Pennsylvania) October 20, 1987
"No Signs of Foul Play," Kologie, Carl, *Indiana Gazette*, (Indiana, Pennsylvania) October 23, 1987
"Mom cites 'tragic example' to peers," Johnson, Robert, *The Pittsburgh Press*, (Pittsburgh, Penns ylvania) October 23, 1987
"He was somebody's son, friend...", Rizzo, Monica, *Indiana Gazette*, (Indiana, Pennsylvania) October 23, 1987

**CHAPTER SIX**
"Charges filed against bartender, local tavern," *Indiana Gazette*, (Indiana, Pennsylvania) February, 17, 1988
"No appeal granted," *Indiana Gazette*, (Indiana, Pennsylvania) June 6. 1989
"LCB Judge voids tavern citations in death," Johnson, Robert, *The Pittsburgh Press*, (Pittsburgh, Pennsylvania) June 23, 1988
"IUP Death/Judge dismisses charges against Indiana tavern," *Indiana Gazette*, (Indiana, Pennsylvania) June 23, 1988

**CHAPTER NINE**
"Capital Campaign exceeds $4 Million," IUP Media Relations, *The Penn*, (Indiana, Pennsylvania) November 4, 1987
"IUP capital fund drive over quota," Orr, Jim, *Indiana Gazette*, (Indiana, Pennsylvania) October 30, 1987
"45 nabbed in district drug bust," *Indiana Gazette*, (Indiana, Pennsylvania) October 6, 1987
"IUP open house attracts students from afar," Barwick, Avril, *Indiana Gazette*, (Indiana, Pennsylvania) October 26, 1987
"IUP initiates ad campaign with Time, Newsweek spots," Ritter, Dawn, *The Penn*, (Indiana, Pennsylvania) September 1987.

CHAPTER FIFTEEN
Transcript, Liquor Control Board Hearing, Capital City Reporting Service, March 20, 1989

CHAPTER NINETEEN
"Death on Campus; PART I; IUP student's death still troubles family," Gentilcore-Brennan, Marlene and Santus, Sharon, *Tribune-Review*, (Greensburg, Pennsylvania) April 29, 1990
"Death on Campus, PART II; Findings disputed in student's death," Gentilcore-Brennan, Marlene and Santus, Sharon, *Tribune-Review*, (Greensburg, Pennsylvania) April 30, 1990
"Death on Campus, PART III; Parents recall agonizing search for son," Gentilcore-Brennan, Marlene and Santus, Sharon, *Tribune-Review*, (Greensburg, Pennsylvania) May 1, 1990

CHAPTER TWENTY
"Indiana officials to re-examine details in IUP student's death," Santus, Sharon, *Tribune-Review*, (Greensburg, Pennsylvania) October 14, 1990
"Inquiry into death of student suspended," Santus, Sharon, *Tribune-Review*, (Greensburg, Pennsylvania) October 16, 1990
"DA upset over publicity suspends new death probe," Wells, Randy, *Indiana Gazette*, (Indiana, Pennsylvania) October 16, 1990
"End the Suspension," Koloski, Paul *Tribune-Review*, (Greensburg, Pennsylvania) October 17, 1990
"Family to ask state to probe into IUP death," Santus, Sharon, *Tribune-Review*, (Greensburg, Pennsylvania) October 17, 1990
"Investigation into student death on again," Santus, Sharon, *Tribune-Review*, (Greensburg, Pennsylvania) October 19, 1990

CHAPTER TWENTY-FIVE
*Unsolved Mysteries*, Cosgrove-Meurer Productions, NBC, January 6, 1995

CHAPTER TWENTY-SIX
"Family of dead student files criminal complaint," Santus, Sharon, *Tribune-Review*, (Greensburg, Pennsylvania) January 14, 1995